W9-CNC-811

CONTENTS

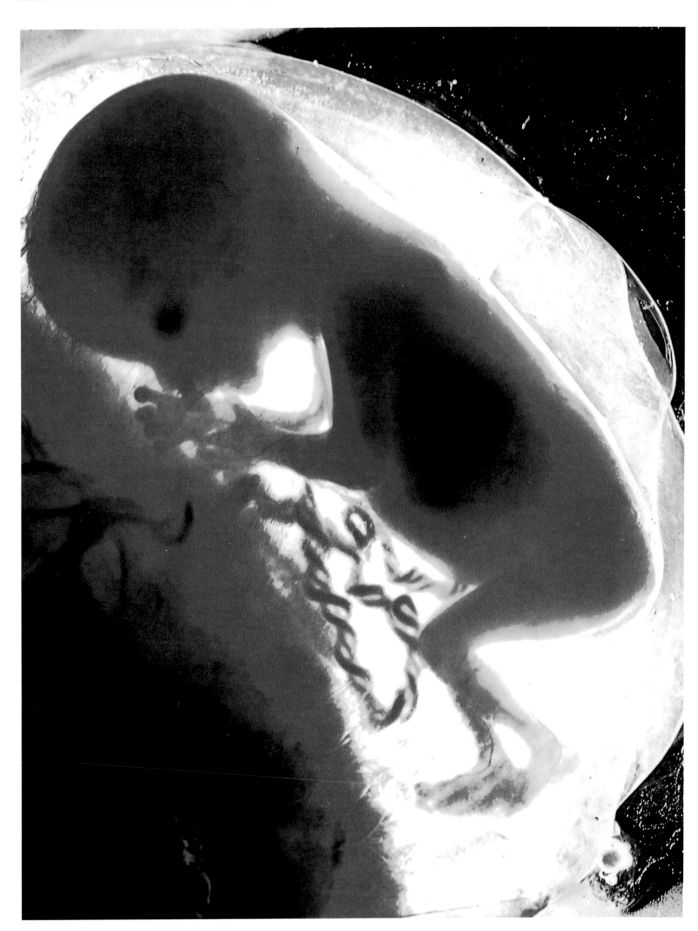

▲ During the **REPRODUCTION** process, vital nourishment passes through the placenta to the fetus.

YOUNG STUDENTS
Learning
Library®

VOLUME 18

Pueblos —
Rome, Ancient

NEWFIELD
PUBLICATIONS
SHELTON, CONNECTICUT

CREDITS

2183 ZEFA; 2185 Kobal Collection; 2188 Peter Newark; 2189 ZEFA; 2193 ZEFA; 2194 ZEFA; 2195 Pat Morris; 2197 Armando Curcio Editore; 2203 Helene Rogers/Trip; 2206 Max Planck Institute for Radio Astronomy; 2207 EPA/Pictorial Parade; 2211 ZEFA; 2219 Hulton; 2225 National Gallery of Art, Washington, D.C. (top), Armando Curcio Editore (bottom); 2226 Library of Congress; 2227 Library of Congress; 2233 Armando Curcio Editore (bottom), Spectrum Colour Library (top); 2234 Giraudon; 2236 Hutchison; 2242 National Gallery of Art, Washington, D.C.; 2243 Armando Curcio Editore; 2244 Armando Curcio Editore; 2246 Armando Curcio Editore; 2252 SATOUR; 2255 ZEFA; 2258 Bettmann Archive; 2260 Connecticut Historical Society; 2264 Armando Curcio Editore (top); Edinburgh University Library (bottom); 2265 ZEFA; 2268 ZEFA (top); Photri (bottom); 2272 British Library; 2273 Armando Curcio Editore; 2274 Hulton; 2275 Texas Highway Dept.; 2277 Armando Curcio Editore; 2280 ZEFA; 2284 ZEFA; 2285 National Gallery of Art, Washington, D.C. (top), Armando Curcio Editore (bottom); 2286 Bulloz (top), Biofotos (bottom); 2289 N.B.C.; 2291 British Museum (center right); 2292 British Museum; 2293 British Museum; 2294 ZEFA; 2297 Armando Curcio Editore (top right), Ronald Sheridan (bottom); 2298 Scala; 2300 National Gallery of Art, Washington, D.C. (top left), Gerhards Heinhold (bottom left); 2301 Picturepoint.

Young Students Learning Library and Newfield Publications are federally registered trademarks of Newfield Publications, Inc.

Copyright © 1994 by Newfield Publications, Inc.; 1974, 1972 by Funk & Wagnalls, Inc. & Newfield Publications, Inc.

Maps containing the appropriate Donnelley indication are copyright © 1994 by R.R. Donnelley and Sons Company. This product contains proprietary property of R. R. Donnelley & Sons Company.

Unauthorized use, including copying, of this product is expressly prohibited.

Printed in the U.S.A.

ISBN 0-8374-9825-2

PUEBLOS

The Pueblos are a group of closely related Native American tribes that live in New Mexico and Arizona. When Spanish explorers arrived in New Mexico in the early 1500s, they found people living there in villages built of *adobe* (sun-dried mud and straw) brick. The Spaniards named them Pueblos, because the word *pueblo* means "village" in Spanish.

The ancestors of the Pueblos were the first people to inhabit the Southwest. They were farmers who grew corn, beans, and cotton. They wove cloth from the cotton and made baskets and pottery. They also hunted for small game. The Pueblos were shorter and darker than their neighbors, the tribes who lived in the Great Plains.

The lives of Pueblo tribes today reflect the ways of their ancestors. Many still live in adobe homes and work as farmers. But the Spanish taught them to raise sheep and cat-

 Tribes such as the Zuni, Hopi, Keresan, and Tanoan built villages of terraced houses called *pueblos*.

tle, and they no longer hunt. Pottery making has become a highly developed art. The two main tribes of the Pueblos are the Hopi and the Zuni.

The Pueblo tribe worship a number of gods of nature. The "Snake Dance" was one of their most important religious ceremonies. Dancers carried live rattlesnakes in their mouths as a kind of prayer for rain.

▶ ▶ ▶ ▶ **FIND OUT MORE** ◀ ◀ ◀ ◀

Cliff Dwellers; Native American Art; Native Americans

PUERTO RICO

The Commonwealth of Puerto Rico is an island in the West Indies with more than three million inhabitants. Its capital and largest city is the beautiful port city of San Juan. The Caribbean Sea lies to the south of Puerto Rico and the Atlantic Ocean is on the north. The island lies about 885 miles (1,425 km) southeast of Florida. Puerto Rico is a commonwealth that governs itself, but it has the military protection and certain economic and political privileges of the United States. Puerto Ricans are U.S. citizens, but they cannot vote for President or members of Congress.

Puerto Rican cities are situated in the coastal lowlands. Farmland is in the nearby valleys. Mountains rise in the south central part of the island. The rain forest on the slopes of the mountain El Yunque, not far from San Juan, sometimes has as much as 200 inches (500 cm) of rainfall a year. Huge tropical trees and exotic flowers grow wild there.

Many Puerto Ricans make their living by farming. Sugarcane, coconuts, pineapples and other fruits, and tobacco are some of the main crops. Livestock and dairy products are important to the economy, too. Puerto Ricans are largely of Spanish descent and most of them speak Spanish. A child's

WHERE TO DISCOVER MORE

Trimble, Stephen. *The Village of Blue Stone.* New York: Macmillan, 1990.

Yue, Charlotte. *The Pueblo.* New York: Houghton Mifflin, 1986.

Children in Puerto Rico celebrate "Three Kings Day" on January 6. They receive gifts on this day as well as on Christmas Day.

PUERTO RICO

Capital city
San Juan
(431,000 people)

Area
3,435 square miles
(8,897 sq. km)

Population
3,316,000 people

Government
Commonwealth
governing part of
United States

Natural resources
Copper, nickel,
potential for oil

Export products
Sugar, coffee,
petroleum products,
chemicals, metal
products, textiles

Unit of money
U.S. dollar

Official languages
Spanish and English

education is mainly in Spanish, although English is taught beginning in the first grade.

Christopher Columbus discovered Puerto Rico in 1493. He named it *San Juan Bautista*, St. John the Baptist. The explorer Ponce de León, claimed the island for Spain in 1509 and started a Spanish settlement. Carib and Arawak tribes were living on the island then. Its rich vegetation and reports of gold made the Spanish call the island Puerto Rico, the "rich port." The gold soon gave out, however, and the island became a Spanish colony of large plantations. Black

moves did not satisfy the Nationalist Party of the country, which led an unsuccessful revolution in 1950. The United States decided to allow the island to draft its own constitution. Puerto Ricans then were allowed to choose among complete independence, full statehood within the United States, or a continuation of commonwealth status. A majority of the voters chose to remain a commonwealth. Puerto Ricans elect their governor and a legislative assembly.

Puerto Rico is a densely populated island. More than one-third of the people live in the six largest cities

slaves brought by the Spaniards from Africa during the 1700s and 1800s were the ancestors of some Puerto Ricans. El Morro, a fortress built by the Spaniards on the Bay of San Juan, still stands. In 1898, Spain granted the island self-rule. Soon after, Puerto Rico was occupied by U.S. troops during the Spanish-American War and eventually given by Spain to the United States.

U.S. citizens soon acquired most of the major plantations, and many Puerto Ricans became restless with what they considered to be second-class status. In 1917, however, the Jones Act passed by the U.S. Congress gave full citizenship to Puerto Ricans and allowed them some self-rule. In 1947, they were allowed to choose their own governor. These

Bayamón, Caguas, Carolina, Mayagüez, Ponce, and San Juan. Overpopulation and high unemployment caused thousands of Puerto Ricans to emigrate to the United States in the 1950s and 1960s. Since about 1975, the island's economy has markedly improved, and Puerto Ricans have found more jobs. "Operation Bootstrap," an economic plan of the Puerto Rican government, encouraged large-scale U.S. investment. The government helped factory owners find locations and train workers. Many U.S. manufacturers opened factories on the island also. Thousands of people are employed in factories that make textiles, chemicals, electrical equipment, and many other products. Other factories process food and refine sugar.

▲ **The Commonwealth of Puerto Rico consists of beautiful islands lying between the Atlantic Ocean in the north and the Caribbean Sea to the south.**

The tropical climate and sandy beaches attract many tourists to Puerto Rico. Frost and snow are unknown on the island, and even hail only occurs rarely. The average temperature in January is about 73°F (23°C). Big hotels have been built in the Condado Beach section of San Juan and in other parts of the island.

▶▶▶▶ **FIND OUT MORE** ◀◀◀◀
Columbus, Christopher;
Spanish-American War

PULLEY

SEE MACHINE

PULSAR

SEE STAR

PULSE

SEE CIRCULATORY SYSTEM

PUMA

SEE CAT, WILD

PUMP

A pump, such as a bicycle pump or an automobile fuel pump is a machine that moves a *fluid* (a liquid or a gas).

A *reciprocating*, or *displacement*, pump works by sucking or pulling fluid into a chamber through an *intake* opening and then pushing it out of the chamber through an *outlet* opening. When you pull up on the handle of a bicycle pump, a *piston* (solid cylinder part) inside the pump moves up and air from outside rushes in through an *intake valve* (an opening with a lid on it). When you press down on the handle, the piston forces the air out through an outlet valve into the bicycle tire. The lids of the two valves open in different directions, so that the air pressure that forces one valve open forces the other valve shut.

▼ In a bicycle pump, (1) air is taken in through a valve by pulling up the plunger. (2) The air is forced out when the plunger is pushed down and air pressure shuts this valve; (3) At the same time, the air is forced through another valve into the inner tube of the tire, which is of a lower pressure. (4) The second valve allows the air to pass into the tire, but does not allow it to pass out again.

Handle

Plunger

Piston

Valve

Plunger movement

Air movement

(1)

(2)

Hose

Inner tube

Tire

Valve

(3)

(4)

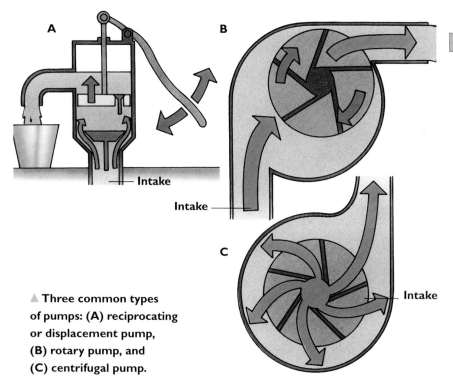

A

B

C

Intake

Intake

Intake

▲ **Three common types of pumps: (A) reciprocating or displacement pump, (B) rotary pump, and (C) centrifugal pump.**

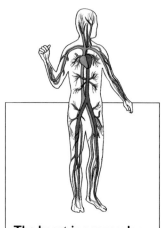

The heart is a muscular pump. The body needs oxygen to live. Blood absorbs oxygen in the lungs. This oxygenated blood is pumped around the body by the heart. The heart consists of four chambers. Valves open and close to allow the blood to pass through the chambers, and to stop it from flowing back again.

This makes sure that the air comes in only through the intake valve and goes out only through the outlet valve.

A *rotary* pump is a kind of displacement pump that doesn't have a piston. Instead, it has a wheel that turns inside. The wheel uncovers the intake and sucks the fluid in. Then it closes the intake and uncovers the outlet and forces the fluid out. Gasoline pumps are rotary pumps. Some rotary pumps have gears inside. The gears catch the fluid from the intake between their teeth and carry it around to the outlet. Gear pumps are very strong. They are used to pump thick liquids, such as oil, in an automobile oil pump.

In a *centrifugal* pump, the fluid comes in through an intake in the middle and is picked up by flat blades that whip it around to the outside and force it through the outlet. To understand this idea better, imagine a fan with flat blades that are positioned so that only the sides of the blades show from the front of the fan. When the fan turns, air is forced from the inside of the fan out, instead of from back to front.

▶▶▶▶ **FIND OUT MORE** ◀◀◀◀
Physics

PUNCTUATION

As you listen to your friends talk, you will notice that their speech is full of little pauses and changes in *pitch* (high, low, or intermediate sounds). These pauses and pitch changes help you understand more easily what your friends are saying. Punctuation marks are the symbols used in written language to indicate the little pauses and changes of pitch that would be heard if you were speaking the words aloud.

HYPHEN (-) A hyphen is a mark used either as a connector or a separator. In some cases hyphens connect the words to suggest a continuous sound, such as "clang-clang-clang." The hyphen is also used for connecting two different words to create a new meaning and at the end of a line to divide a word that is to be continued on the next line.

Example: 555-1234
Example: Spanish-speaking.
Example: It will be better to arrive at suppertime.

PERIOD (.) A period is a full-stop punctuation mark. In written language, a period is placed where the sound of the voice would stop if the sentence were spoken aloud.

SEMICOLON (;) Another full-stop mark is the semicolon. It marks a logical break in the progress of a sentence. It is often used to connect the two main clauses of a compound sentence when a conjunction, such as "and," is not used. (I couldn't sleep; I woke up at midnight.) When a conjunction is used between the main clauses, a semicolon is used if the main clauses contain commas. Semicolons are also used to separate items in a series when the items are very long or when other punctuation, such as a comma, is used within the items.

Example: On our trip west, we stopped at Portland, Eugene, and

Myrtle Point in Oregon; Crescent City, Eureka, and Sausalito in California; and Phoenix in Arizona.

APOSTROPHE (') An apostrophe and the letter "s" are usually added to a noun when ownership *(possession)* is shown, as in "the city's night noises." When a plural noun ends in "s," only the apostrophe is necessary to show possession. The apostrophe is also the mark used when joining two words together in a contraction.

Example: They held a teachers' meeting.

Example: I + am = I'm

QUOTATION MARKS (" ") When indicating exactly what someone said, or when quoting from something that has been written, quotation marks are used at the beginning and at the end of the quotation. When someone is being quoted within the quotation, single quotation marks ('...') are used.

Example: Anne said, "He told me, 'I left it in the desk drawer.'"

EXCLAMATION POINT (!) The exclamation point is used to express emotion or show emphasis.

Example: Look out!

COMMA (,) The comma makes reading easier, just as pausing to breathe makes speaking easier. As a punctuation mark, the comma indicates a brief pause in the flow of a sentence or some portion of it. Commas are also used to separate the items of a series when the items themselves do not contain commas.

Example: When you get a flat tire, it helps to have a spare, a jack, a lug wrench, and someone to help you change the tire.

QUESTION MARK (?) The question mark is used at the end of any words phrased as a question. Otherwise, the meaning would be different.

Example: He's coming, too?
He's coming, too.

COLON (:) The colon usually indicates a longer pause than the comma and semicolon. It is often used before a list of items. It shows that what follows is in some way connected with what went before. Colons are also used after the salutation of a business letter

Example: At the zoo, I saw many animals: lions, bears, and monkeys.

Example: Dear Dr. Jones:
I will see you at 2:30 p.m.

PARENTHESES [( )] Parentheses indicate an interruption and set of additional words, explanation, or comment that is helpful but not really necessary to the meaning of the sentence.

Example: The chairs (but not the tables) can be moved easily.

DASH (—) The function of a single dash is somewhat like that of the comma or colon. A pair of dashes is used in the same way that parentheses are used.

Example: John—who teaches physical education—is also the Little League coach.

For more details on the functions of each kind of punctuation mark, ask your teacher or consult a grammar textbook.

▶▶▶▶ **FIND OUT MORE** ◀◀◀◀
Abbreviation; Grammar;
Parts of Speech;

PUPPET

The word *puppet* comes from the Latin word *pupa*, meaning "doll." A puppet is a doll that is made to move. You have probably seen puppets on television, such as the "Muppets" of *Sesame Street*. In the past, children enjoyed the television puppets on the

▲ **Kermit the frog, one of Jim Henson's Muppets, is a favorite TV character and movie puppet enjoyed by children and adults.**

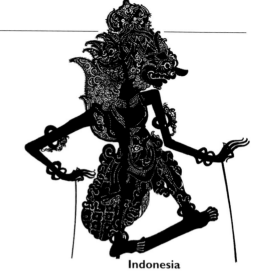

Indonesia

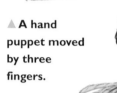

▲ **A hand puppet moved by three fingers.**

▲ **A puppet made from a wooden spoon that has been painted and dressed.**

WHERE TO DISCOVER MORE

Renfro, Nancy. *Puppet Show Made Easy!* New York: Nancy Renfro Studios, 1984.

Paterson, Katherine. *The Master Puppeteer.* New York: Crowell, 1976.

Howdy Doody and the *Kukla, Fran, and Ollie* shows and Shari Lewis's puppets, Lamb Chop, Hush Puppy, and Charlie Horse, who are still performing today.

There are six basic kinds of puppets. A *hand puppet* is worn over the hand, like a mitten. The forefinger is placed in the neck to operate the head. The thumb and middle finger operate the arms. A person, called a *puppeteer*, works the hand puppet from a position behind and below the stage.

A *rod* or *stick puppet* is also operated from beneath the stage. With one hand, the puppeteer holds the puppet's body upright with a rod. With the other hand, he or she moves rods attached to the puppet's arms and head. The rods are in the back of the puppet and cannot be seen by the audience unless the puppet is accidentally turned around.

Shadow puppets are actually rod puppets. Instead of watching the puppets directly, the audience watches a screen on which the puppets' shadows are cast. Some shadow puppets are made of colorful, translucent materials, such as glass or plastic. The light shines through these materials so that color as well as shape can be seen on the screen. Shadow puppets can be turned in almost any direction, because the audience never sees the rods that work them.

To operate *finger puppets*, the puppeteer's middle finger and forefinger become the puppet's legs. Tiny shoes are worn on the fingertips, and the puppet's upper body is strapped to the top of the puppeteer's hand. With the free hand, the puppeteer uses strings to operate the head and arms. When working a finger puppet, the puppeteer's hand must be on stage. The puppeteer usually wears black, long-sleeved clothing during a

Greece

China

▲ **A collection of puppets from around the world. Puppets are often part of religious festivals.**

performance so his or her presence will not be so noticeable.

A *ventriloquist* is someone who has learned to speak without moving the lips. He or she holds a *dummy* (a large doll), placing one hand in the dummy's back to operate the head, eyes, mouth, and arms. During a performance, the ventriloquist, without moving his or her own lips, makes the dummy move and speak so that it seems as if the dummy were talking. One of the most famous ventriloquists was Edgar Bergen whose dummy was a fast-talking wise guy, Charlie McCarthy.

Marionettes are string-operated puppets. The puppeteer stands above and behind the stage, controlling the marionette with as many as 30 strings. Simpler marionettes are made with seven strings running to the hands, knees, sides of the head, and back of the puppet.

Recently, an electrically operated, remote-control puppet has been invented. This kind of puppet is able to move around a stage without the aid of strings or a puppeteer's hand. The puppet's body is made of soft materials that allow the puppeteer to control its movements.

No one knows exactly where or when puppets originated. The ancient Hindus of India believed that puppets were friends of gods. Ancient Egyptians had puppets, representing spirits and gods, which were carried in religious processions. Puppet plays were a favorite form of entertainment in ancient China, Japan, Greece, Rome, and Indonesia.

During the Middle Ages, Italian puppeteers gave performances throughout Europe. Puppet plays were presented on tiny stages set up in buildings or on street corners. Most early European puppet plays were based on religious or Biblical stories. During the 1300s and 1400s, fables and comedies became popular. One of the favorite puppet characters of those days was *Pulcinella*, who was portrayed as a flirt and prankster. In France, Pulcinella became *Polichinelle*, and in Spain the character became known as *Don Cristobal Pulchinela*. The French Polichinelle was taken to England in 1662, where he became known as *Punch*. English puppeteers gave Punch a wife named Judy. The famous "Punch and Judy Shows" have amused audiences in Europe and the United States for many years. In Italy and other countries, *Pinocchio* (a puppet who turns into a boy) became another favorite character. A favorite German puppet was *Hans Wurst* (John Sausage), and in the Netherlands *Jan Pickel Herringe* (John Pickled Herring) was a popular puppet.

▶ **Puppeteers who use string puppets have to have very nimble fingers. Each string moves a different part of the puppet's body. Often several parts have to be moved at once to make the puppet look more real.**

Puppetry is a form of drama, and in many areas of the world it has developed into a great art. In Asia, puppeteers have created elaborate, complicated puppets that wear beautifully decorated costumes. In China and Indonesia, *shadow plays* (in which puppets are operated behind lighted, transparent curtains) have been popular for centuries. Puppeteers from all over the world come to train at the Central State Puppet Theater in Moscow in Russia. The Teatro del Nahuatl in Mexico City is also one of the world's great puppet theaters.

▶▶▶▶**FIND OUT MORE**◀◀◀◀
Actors and Acting; Doll; Drama

LEARN BY DOING

You can make a hand puppet of your own, using an old sock. Decide where you want the eyes and nose, and sew buttons on for each. Yarn or scraps of material can be glued or sewn on to make hair, eyebrows, a beard, costumes, or other kinds of decorations. Give your puppet a voice and practice making its actions fit the words as you speak them.

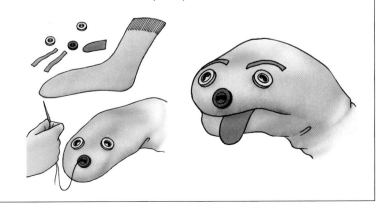

PURITAN

About 400 years ago, many Protestants in England were known as Puritans, because they wished to "purify" the services of the Church of England. Puritans wanted to do away

▲ Many of the first European colonists were people who disagreed with the accepted religion in their own country and who were persecuted for their beliefs. The English Puritans were one such group. Many settled in America.

with elaborate *rituals*. They emphasized preaching rather than sacraments. All English people, however, were expected to worship God in the manner decided by the king and church authorities. The Puritans, who refused, were severely punished. Many felt it was dangerous to remain in their native land, and they decided to seek freedom in America.

In 1629, a group of Puritans formed the Massachusetts Bay Company. The king gave them a charter granting them permission to settle on land not far from Plymouth, a town founded by the Pilgrims in 1620. The Puritans landed in the New World and named their settlement Boston.

During the next few years, other Puritans crossed the Atlantic and started new towns. The people who settled all important matters in the colony had to be members of the Puritan church, and anyone who disagreed with them ran the risk of harsh punishment. One form of punishment was putting people in *stocks*, a wood frame with holes for confining the ankles, wrists, and sometimes the head. (The person being punished would be put in stocks in a public place to shame him or her.) The Puritans had come to the New World to find religious freedom, but they were not willing to give the same freedom to others.

Many Puritans who wanted real religious freedom left and started new settlements. Roger Williams founded what is now Rhode Island, and Thomas Hooker founded what is now Connecticut.

Puritans who remained in England supported the civil war that started in 1642 and ended with the beheading of King Charles I in 1649. (These Puritans were called Roundheads, because they cut their hair short.) They established a commonwealth led by Oliver Cromwell in 1649. After disagreements within the government, the commonwealth was ended. A Protectorate was established with Cromwell as the absolute ruler. The Puritan government was tolerant of most Protestant religions but no others. It forced a very strict morality on English life. In 1660, the monarchy was reestablished. The Puritans were then treated even more harshly than they had been before the revolution. Many years passed before Puritans in England gained full religious freedom and all their civil rights.

▶ ▶ ▶ ▶ **FIND OUT MORE** ◀ ◀ ◀ ◀
Connecticut; Cromwell, Oliver; English History; Massachusetts; Pilgrim Settlers; Rhode Island; Williams, Roger

WHERE TO DISCOVER MORE

Alderman, Clifford Lindsey. *The Story of the Thirteen Colonies.* New York: Random House, 1966.
Siegel, Beatrice. *A New Look at the Pilgrims: Why They Came to America.* New York: Walker & Co., 1977.

PYGMY

A *Pygmy*, or Pigmy, is a member of any of several short peoples who live in parts of Africa and Asia. The word pygmy refers generally to someone or something small. Pygmies range from 4 to 5 feet (1.2 to 1.5 m) in height. They have a lighter skin color than many black people have. Some *anthropologists* (scientists who study human cultures) consider the Pygmies part of the Negroid race, but others believe they are a separate race.

African Pygmies, sometimes called *Negrillos,* live in the dense tropical jungles and rain forests of Burundi, Cameroon, Congo, Gabon, Rwanda, and Zaire. African Pygmies live in groups of about 20 families. They hunt and gather honey, fruit, and vegetables. They use nets to trap animals and then kill them with spears or bows and arrows, often poison-tipped. This method enables Pygmies to kill even very large animals, such as antelopes and buffaloes. Pygmies *migrate* (move) often from place to place within the jungle in search of fresh game. They live in huts made of twigs and leaves. Pygmies trade with African villagers who live near them.

Asian Pygmies, sometimes called *Negritos,* live in southeastern Asia, mainly on the Malay Peninsula and the Philippine and Andaman islands. Their skin color may range from yellow to black (African Pygmies usually have a reddish brown skin), and their hair may be thick and long (African Pygmies usually have short, curly hair). Some Asian Pygmies now live permanently in one place and farm or work as laborers.

Most Pygmy populations are declining because of interbreeding with other groups, low birth rates, and high infant death rates. Pygmies may possibly become extinct in the near future.

▶ ▶ ▶ ▶ **FIND OUT MORE** ◀ ◀ ◀ ◀
Africa; Growth; Jungle; Pacific Islands

PYRAMID

In geometry, a *pyramid* is a solid shape with a many-sided base and triangular sides sloping up to a common point. In architecture, a pyramid is a large structure with the same shape. Most of these pyramids are made of stone and have a square base and four sides. Sometimes the sides are stepped.

Pyramids have been built in many parts of the world. The most famous pyramids are those of ancient Egypt. About 4,500 years ago, an Egyptian *pharaoh* (king) named Zoser ordered the first pyramid built as a burial tomb. Until that time, most Egyptians had built small mudbrick tombs called *mastabas.* Zoser's Step Pyramid at Saqqara (near Cairo) was the world's first all-stone structure. It was called a "step pyramid," because it rose in levels like huge stepping-stones. Later, the pharaohs Cheops, Khafre, and Menkaure built three massive pyramids at Giza. Cheops' Great Pyramid was the first, taking about 20 years to complete. It was originally 481 feet (147 m) high, and

▲ A pygmy of the Bambuti tribe that lives in the forests of Zaire.

▼ The great pyramids at Giza in Egypt are an awesome achievement, even judged by today's advanced engineering methods.

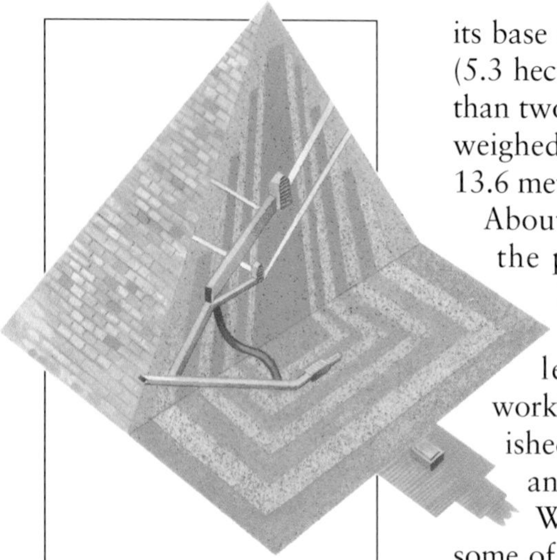

The first people to use geometry were the Babylonians and the Ancient Egyptian pyramid builders more than 5,000 years ago.

▼ The Egyptians were not the only ancient civilization to build pyramids. Between A.D. 300 and 900 the Mayas of Central America built huge pyramids and temples for the purpose of worship.

its base covered more than 13 acres (5.3 hectares). It was made of more than two million stone blocks. They weighed from 2 to 15 tons (1.8 to 13.6 metric tons) each.

About 4,000 persons worked on the project at one time. They hauled the great stone blocks up dirt ramps to the level on which they were working. When that level was finished, they built a higher ramp and started on the next level. When the top was reached, some of the stones were evened off. Facing stones were carefully added to fill in the spaces. When it was completed, the pyramid looked like a solid piece of stone. Today, many of the facing stones have disappeared, and the sides of the pyramids look as if they are covered with huge stone steps. Inside the pyramid were the pharaoh's burial chamber and many other rooms filled with marvelous treasures for a dead pharaoh's soul to use in the next life. After the burial, the entrances to these chambers were sealed with huge stones. But most pyramids were later broken into and robbed of their treasures. The ruins of about 80 pyramids remain today in Egypt.

The natives of Central America and Mexico also built great stepped temples that were like pyramids. These pyramids often had flat terraces cut into their sides and flat tops on which temples were built. The Pyramid of the Sun at Teotihuacán near Mexico City has a larger base than any Egyptian pyramid.

▶ ▶ ▶ ▶ **FIND OUT MORE** ◀ ◀ ◀ ◀
Egypt, Ancient; Maya

PYTHAGORAS
(about 570–500 B.C.)

Very little is known about the life of this great Greek thinker. He is said to have traveled in Egypt and the Far East. We know that he moved from the island of Samos, in the Mediterranean Sea, to Croton, Italy, in 529 B.C. At Croton, he founded a cult that was part scientific, part religious. He thought he was a *demigod* (half-god, half-human).

Pythagoras's most important ideas were about geometry and about sound. His best-known work in geometry has come down to us as the *Pythagorean Theorem*. It states that the square of the *hypotenuse* (long side) of a right triangle is equal to the sum of the squares of the other two sides (see the diagram below).

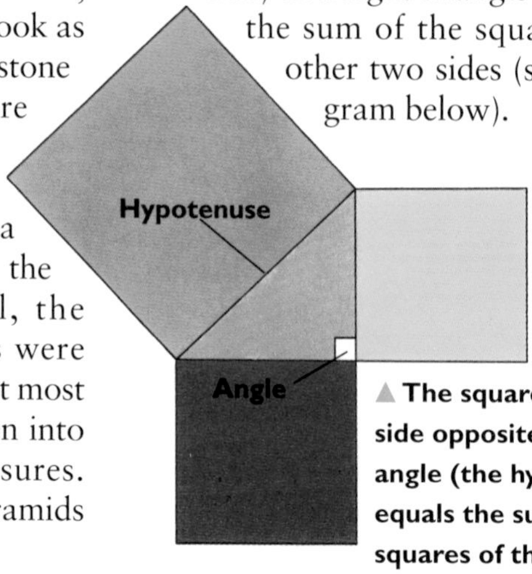

Hypotenuse

Angle

▲ The square on the side opposite the right angle (the hypotenuse) equals the sum of the squares of the other two sides.

In the field of music, Pythagoras observed that the string of a musical instrument vibrates to produce a sound. He noticed that a string half the length, but at the same *tautness* (tension), produces a note an octave higher. He found other simple fractions of the string's length produced musical harmonies.

He and his followers believed that numbers and music were the most important things in the universe. They thought, for example, that the planets made music as they moved.

▶ ▶ ▶ ▶ **FIND OUT MORE** ◀ ◀ ◀ ◀
Geometry; Music; Sound

QATAR

SEE ASIA

QUAKERS

SEE SOCIETY OF FRIENDS

QUANTUM

When you look at the light coming from an electric light bulb, it seems to be steady and unwavering. Actually, light is not as steady as it seems. It is given off in a vast number of tiny packages of energy, like the bullets from a machine gun. Each of these packages is called a *quantum* (plural: *quanta*). The quantum is a very small, but definite, amount of energy.

Sometimes we think of light and other forms of energy, such as radio waves and X rays, as traveling in reg-

ular waves. The brightness of the light depends on the height of the waves. The color of the light depends on the distance between the waves.

Light can also be thought of as a stream of quantum particles or individual *photons*. The energy of each photon depends on the wavelength and therefore the color of the light. A photon of white light has more energy than a photon of red light. This explains why a piece of iron glows first red, then yellow, and finally white when heated in a fire. As it gets hotter, it takes in more energy and gives out waves or photons of greater energy. Scientists today think of light as having either wavelike properties or particlelike (photon) properties, depending on the methods used to measure them. This is called *wave-particle duality*.

▶▶▶▶ **FIND OUT MORE** ◀◀◀◀
Atom; Einstein, Albert; Physics; Planck, Max; Spectrum

QUARK

SEE NUCLEAR ENERGY AND PARTICLE PHYSICS

QUARRYING

Quarrying is the mining of rock or stone from large open *quarries*, or pits. As large amounts of stone are removed from the earth, the deep hole that is made is called the quarry. Marble, slate, granite, and limestone are the chief kinds of rock that are quarried for all kinds of uses.

Egg-sized pieces of rock called *trap*, or *traprock*, are used as foun-

Energy

Electron

1

Electron

Normal orbit

Nucleus

High orbit

2

Electromagnetic radiation given out

▲ When an atom absorbs energy, one of its electrons moves into a higher orbit (1). On its return, it emits the same energy as a photon of radiation (2).

DEVELOPMENT OF THE LETTER Q

The Egyptian Q
c. 3000 B.C.

The Phoenician Q
c. 1500 B.C.

The Greek Q
c. 800 B.C.

The modern Q from the Roman

▲ Rock is quarried for many uses: In the quarry, (1) workers prepare for blasting. Dynamite or other explosives break up the rock (2), and diggers (3) load it into trucks for transporting (4) to the crushing plant (5). There, the rock is broken down even more for use on rail lines (6), road beds (7), and as cement for concrete buildings (8).

The largest modern quarry is Bingham Canyon Copper Mine in Utah. This quarry covers 2.8 square miles (7.2 sq. km) and is 2,500 feet (760 m) deep.

dations on which to build highways and railroads. To quarry rocks of this size, *blasting* is done. Holes are drilled into the rock, and sticks of dynamite are put into the holes. The exploding dynamite shatters the rock into small pieces. The blasted pieces are scooped up and sorted for size. Those that are too big are put into crushing machines that break them into smaller pieces.

Building stones are used for large buildings and the foundations of bridges. These stones are quarried in large unbroken blocks or slabs. One way to cut blocks of stone is to drill a row of holes in the rock and insert special wedges into the holes. Workers hammer on the whole row of wedges at the same time. This splits off a slab of rock. Sometimes explosives are used to loosen the stone.

Channeling machines and *wire saws* are used to quarry soft stones, such as limestone and sandstone. A channeling machine looks somewhat like a small locomotive. It moves along a track. Attached to its side are long chisels or very tough saws. Both are moved by steam power. The channeling machine cuts long vertical channels deep into the stone. Then, a *gadding machine*, similar to a channeling machine, cuts a horizontal channel. This frees the block of stone. A wire saw has an endless,

tough steel wire revolving on two pulleys at the ends of a steel shaft. An *abrasive*, a gritty substance such as sand, is poured on the wire as it runs. The wire rubs across the rock and cuts it. When all of the useful stone has been taken out of the ground, quarries are abandoned. Abandoned quarries often fill up with water and become deep pools.

▶▶▶▶ **FIND OUT MORE** ◀◀◀◀
Granite; Mines and Mining; Rock

QUASAR

SEE RADIO ASTRONOMY

QUEBEC

Quebec is Canada's largest province and the one where many people speak French. Its area is slightly larger than that of Alaska, and its population is more than a fourth of the Canadian total. Ontario and Hudson Bay border Quebec on the west, and Newfoundland-Labrador on the east. New Brunswick and some of the northeastern United States are to the south. The St. Lawrence River flows through southeastern Quebec.

The Land and Climate
Except for the broad, fertile lowlands beside the St. Lawrence River, Quebec is largely a hilly province, two-thirds of which is covered with forests and dotted with thousands of lakes and rivers. The Laurentian Mountains, or the *Laurentides*, are in southern Quebec.

The climate ranges from Arctic temperatures in the far northern Ungava Peninsula to more moderate temperatures in the south. Most areas have a snowfall of more than 100 inches (250 cm) a year with snow on the ground from November to April.

Ivujivik
Kangiqsujuaq
Povungnituk
Povungnituk R.
UNGAVA PENINSULA
Hudson Strait
Ungava Bay
Inukjuak
HUDSON BAY
R. aux Feuilles
Kuujjuaq
Mont D'Iberville
5,422 ft.
1,652 m.
George R.
Caniapiscau R.
à l'Eau Claire
Pt. Louis XIV
Grande R. de la Baleine
L. Bienville
L. Caniapiscau
Baleine R.
Scheffervile
Chisasibi
La Grande R.
James Bay
Eastmain R.
Fermont
Rupert R.
Ontario R.
Manicouagan Res.
L. Mistassini
Betsiamites R.
Havre-St.-Pierre
Sept-Îles
Jacques Cartier Passage
Anticosti I.
Chibougamau
La Sarre
Gouin Res.
L. St. Jean
Baie-Comeau
Gaspé Peninsula Mts.
Gaspé
Gulf of St. Lawrence
Rouyn-Noranda
Alma
Rimouski
Percé
Val-d'Or
Chicoutimi
St. Maurice R.
Notre Dame
Cabonga Res.
Rivière-du-Loup
La Tuque
Madeleine Is.
Ottawa R.
Maniwaki
Shawinigan
Montmagny
Québec
Trois-Rivières
Drummondville
Hull
Sherbrooke
Montréal

N W E S

0   200   400 Miles
0   200   400   600 Kilometers
© 1994 GeoSystems, an R.R. Donnelley & Sons Company

▼ **The Château Frontenac rises majestically over the St. Lawrence River. Its red brick towers and steep copper roofs give a very European feel to this part of Quebec City.**

QUEBEC

Capital
Quebec City
(622,000 people)

Area
594,860 square miles
(1,540,568 sq. km)

Population
1,648,000 people

Entry into confederation
July 1, 1867

Principal river
St. Lawrence

Highest point
Mt. D'Iberville
5,422 feet (1,652 m)

Largest city
Montreal (3,068,000 people in urban area)

Famous people
Saul Bellow, William Shatner, Pierre Trudeau

▶ **The provincial flower of Quebec is the beautiful *Fleur de Lys*, meaning "flower of the lily."**

▲ Boats in the harbor of a fishing village in Quebec. Forests such as those in the background supply lumber for paper mills all over the North American continent.

▼ Quebec City (with the Château Frontenac in the background) is the center of French Canada. Ninety-six percent of the people there speak French.

History

Various Native North American tribes, such as the Micmac, Naskapi, and Algonkian, lived in the Quebec area when the French explorer Jacques Cartier landed on the Gaspé Peninsula in 1534 and claimed the area for France. Another French explorer, Samuel de Champlain, established a settlement on the site of present-day Quebec City in 1608. The area became known as New France. After the British general James Wolfe captured Quebec City in 1759, the area became a British colony. The Quebec Act of 1774 tried to unite the British and French in the colony. The French retained their language, religion, and customs. Quebec became known as Lower Canada in 1791. In 1867, Quebec joined three other colonies to form the new nation of Canada.

English-speaking merchants and manufacturers soon took over financial control of the province. French Canadians centered their lives around their local churches and favored a farming and fishing way of life. The schools provided French-Canadians almost no training for business or industry. Then, in the 1960s, a "quiet revolution" began to take place in Quebec. Education was modernized and made compulsory for everybody. The government started development projects.

French-Canadians demanded that French become the language of business and industry in their province. Many of them wanted Quebec to *secede* (withdraw) from Canada and form a separate nation. The Parti Québécois, a separatist political party, was formed in 1968. French became the province's official language in 1974, and the Parti Québécois gained control of Quebec's legislature in 1976. Montreal is today the second largest French-speaking city in the world. Quebec's "separateness" remains a thorny problem for Canadian unity.

Industry

Quebec is Canada's leading supplier of iron and asbestos and is a good source of copper, zinc, and gold. The waterpower resources of the province are being harnessed by such projects as the Shipshaw hydroelectric plant on the Saguenay River. Forests supply much of the newsprint and wood products used in Canada and the United States.

Visitors to the city of Quebec will see the only "walled city" in North America. The city is divided into an upper and lower town; the upper town is surrounded by heavy walls built by the British in the 1800s. North of Montreal are the Laurentian ski resorts and popular recreation areas.

▶▶▶▶ **FIND OUT MORE** ◀◀◀◀
Canada; Montreal; St. Lawrence Seaway

 ## QUICKSAND

Quicksand is a loose mass of sand that is very wet and behaves like a liquid. The more water it contains, the less weight it can carry and objects will sink into it. However, stories of people being swallowed up by quicksand are probably exaggerated. Water and sand together will support more weight than water alone, and if a person who fell into quicksand kept still, it is unlikely that he or she would sink completely and drown.

Quicksands can form in places where water is prevented from draining away from loose sand. This can happen near the mouths of large rivers, where springs rise up into sand. Quicksands are smaller and much less widespread than has been often speculated. They are, however, a definite hazard in some areas and precautions should be taken to stay clear of them.

▶▶▶▶ **FIND OUT MORE** ◀◀◀◀
Geology; Sand

RABBITS AND HARES

It is easy to confuse rabbits and hares. Why? Because the two animals are alike in many ways. Both have long ears and stubby tails. Both are good jumpers. Both are mammals. But the hare has longer ears and longer hind legs than the rabbit. Hares like to live alone, while two or three rabbit families may live together. Also, rabbits like to live in large *burrows,* or underground shelters. Hares prefer to live above ground, although a hare might hide in another animal's burrow.

Both rabbits and hares are shy, timid creatures. They are the *prey* (hunted victims) of many animals, including human beings. Hares and rabbits are always on the watch for their enemies. The position of their eyes allow them to see what is going on behind and above them.

Rabbits and hares have sharp front teeth for biting into and gnawing on vegetables. They also have flat, ridged back teeth that grind up tough plant material. The teeth keep growing throughout the animals' lives but are worn down by use.

Hares

The hare best known in the United States is called the jackrabbit. It can grow up to 25 inches (65 cm) long and weigh from 8 to 10 pounds (3.5 to 4.5 kg). The jackrabbit lives in the Midwest and West. It can run as fast as 45 miles (72 km) an hour to escape its ene-

▲ **The common rabbit, snug in its burrow made of grass.**

mies. It can even swim across rivers. The jackrabbit hides most of the day under bushes. It comes out only at night to eat grass, but it will eat any kind of vegetable or grain it can find. It especially likes garden vegetables and corn. The jackrabbit can be a great pest to farmers.

A male jackrabbit is called a *buck*. A female is called a *doe*. The doe can have babies about four times a year. She may have as many as four at a time. The young are born with full coats of hair and with their eyes open. The doe feeds her children for about two weeks. She then leaves the young jackrabbits to take care of themselves.

◀ **The snowshoe hare has two coats, one for summer and one for winter.**

DEVELOPMENT OF THE LETTER R

The Semitic R
c. 1500 B.C.

The Phoenician R
c. 1000 B.C.

The Greek R
c. 600 B.C.

The modern R from the Roman

The brown hare found in Europe is often known as the "mad" March hare. It gets its name from the behavior of the male hares in Spring. They chase each other about, leaping high into the air. Sometimes they even have what look like boxing matches, when they stand on their hind legs and spar with their front paws.

▶ The eastern or Florida cottontail, found east of the Rocky Mountains, usually lives on open land.

▲ This dog shows the characteristic signs of an animal infected by rabies. It is baring its teeth and foaming at the mouth.

Rabbits

Like the hare, the rabbit usually comes out to eat grass and other plants at night. It also eats vegetables and grain. The rabbit is always on the lookout for danger. If it sees any enemies about, it thumps a hind leg hard against the ground. The noise warns other rabbits.

The cottontail rabbit is commonly found in the eastern part of the United States. It is usually about 16 to 17 inches (40 to 43 cm) long and weighs about 3 pounds (1.4 kg).

A female cottontail has babies up to eight times a year. The mother may have as many as ten babies at a time. The doe gives birth to her young in a special nest she builds in the ground. The young rabbits are born blind and without any fur on their bodies. When they are about three weeks old, they are old enough to take care of themselves.

Rabbits may make gentle, affectionate pets. They are clean and easy to care for.

▶▶▶▶ **FIND OUT MORE** ◀◀◀◀
Animal; Animal Defenses;
Animal Distribution; Animal Homes;
Animal Tracks; Mammal; Pet

RABIES

Rabies is a virus. It attacks the nervous system of warm-blooded animals, including human beings. The virus can be passed from one animal to another in saliva. This is usually done through a bite by the infected animal. An animal or a human being infected with rabies will die, unless prompt medical treatment is given.

If you are ever attacked and bitten by a dog or a cat that is frothing at the mouth, or if you are bitten by a wild animal, such as a squirrel, bat, skunk, or raccoon, you must act quickly. Call a doctor and the police. Try to keep an eye on the animal that bit you so that the police or dog catcher can capture it. When caught, the animal will be tested to find out whether it has rabies. This is done to find out whether you must be given injections of rabies vaccine so you won't get the disease.

Rabies is also called *hydrophobia*, which means "fear of water." This name was given because animals infected with rabies have swollen throat muscles that contract painfully when the thirsty, infected animal tries to drink water.

▶▶▶▶ **FIND OUT MORE** ◀◀◀◀
Pasteur, Louis;
Veterinary Medicine; Virus

RACCOON

The raccoon is one of the easiest animals to recognize. It looks as if it is wearing a mask across its eyes, and its furry tail has rings around it. The raccoon lives in the woods of the United States and Canada. It likes to live near water because it can swim as well as climb trees. The raccoon usually sleeps all day long in the hollow of a tree. It comes out at night to eat.

Raccoons eat fruits, nuts, roots, chickens, mice and other small forest animals, fish, and even snakes. They are "fishers" by instinct. This is why a caged raccoon will often dip dry food in its water bowl before eating it.

A mother raccoon has babies about once every year. Usually the mother has four babies at a time. The young stay with their mother until they are 1 year old. Then they can hunt food for themselves. Northern raccoons are *partial hibernators*—that is, they go to sleep for long peri-

▲ Raccoons can use their front paws like human hands to hold food and to manipulate objects. Some people think that raccoon tracks look very much like tiny human footprints.

ods in the winter and may wake up on warm winter days and search for food. Raccoons usually live from 10 to 15 years.

▶▶▶ **FIND OUT MORE** ◀◀◀
Animal Distribution; Animal Homes; Animal Tracks

RACE, HUMAN

SEE HUMAN BEING

RACES

SEE MARATHON RACE, TRACK AND FIELD

RACHMANINOFF, SERGEI (1873–1943)

Sergei Vasilyevich Rachmaninoff was a Russian musician who won fame both as a concert pianist and as a composer. He was also a fine orchestra conductor.

Rachmaninoff was born on his family's estate near Novgorod, Russia. He studied music on a scholarship at the St. Petersburg Conser-

vatory and later at the Moscow Conservatory. He met the great Russian composer Peter Tchaikovsky in Moscow. Tchaikovsky's works influenced Rachmaninoff's style.

Rachmaninoff's first symphony was so severely criticized that he stopped composing for a time. But he later wrote two other symphonies that were successful. Four concertos for piano and orchestra also brought him fame. Many pianists play his preludes and other piano solo pieces. Rachmaninoff's music has a powerful, brooding quality.

This talented musician was an exciting pianist to hear. He performed on many concert tours, mostly playing his own works and those of Frédéric Chopin. Rachmaninoff left Russia in 1917 and never went back. Later, the United States became his permanent home. He became a citizen of the United States shortly before his death in 1943.

▶▶▶ **FIND OUT MORE** ◀◀◀
Composer; Music; Piano; Tchaikovsky, Peter

▲ Sergei Rachmaninoff, the famous Russian composer.

▽ The ball used in racquetball is very bouncy, so rallies last a long time. Players need to be able to think and react quickly.

RACQUETBALL

Racquetball is an indoor ball game played rather like handball, but to hit the ball, the players use a racket (racquet) rather than their hands. The racket looks something like a small tennis racket.

Racquetball is a fast game that demands agility and speed. The players hit the ball, which is hollow and made of rubber, against the four walls and ceiling of the court. Two (singles) or four (doubles) may play. The game begins when the player on one side serves by dropping the ball and hitting it on the first bounce against the front wall of the court. It must then be returned by the player

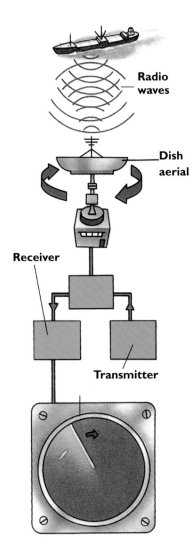

▲ **Radar works by sending out radio signals that bounce off distant objects. The returning signals are decoded by the receiver and produce a picture on the screen showing the position of the objects.**

or team on the other side before it bounces twice on the floor. The ball may hit the ceiling or any one of the walls, but it must hit the front wall before it touches the floor.

Points are scored by the serving side when the opposing side fails to return the ball. This continues as long as the serving side makes no error. When the serving side fails to serve or return properly, it loses the serve to the opposing side. The first player or team to score 21 points wins a game, and the first to win two games wins the match.

▶▶▶▶ **FIND OUT MORE** ◀◀◀◀
Sports

RADAR

When waves hit something solid, they bounce back. If you shout into a well, or into the mouth of a cave, the sound waves of your voice bounce back as an echo. Radar, short for *RAdio Detection And Ranging*, bounces radio waves off objects to find out where the objects are and where they are going.

A radar unit has an *antenna* (used for sending and receiving waves), a *transmitter,* and a *receiver.* The transmitter sends out a *wave pulse* (a short bundle of waves). Radio waves travel at close to 186,000 miles (299,330 km) a second, so it doesn't take them long to get somewhere and back. When the waves hit a solid object, they bounce back to the radar unit.

The radar unit alternately switches off its transmitter and switches on its receiver. The transmitter and the receiver both use the same antenna, so they can't operate at the same time. The receiver picks up the returning waves and sends a signal to an indicator. The most common indicator is a *cathode ray tube,* an electronic tube having a screen much like a television screen. Objects appear as bright spots on the face of the tube. Lines on the tube show the distance and direction of the object.

Radar can also show how fast an object moves. When the waves bounce back from the object, their *frequency* (the number of waves per second) is changed, and the amount of change shows the speed. Some radar systems use continuous waves instead of pulses for this. Then, a separate antenna must be used in addition to the transmitter.

Since radar uses radio waves, it can "see" anywhere radio waves can go. In weather detection, radar can see through clouds and darkness to pick up rain and other kinds of "solid" bad weather.

Radar was developed during World War II as an aid in tracking airplanes and finding targets. This is still one of the most important uses of radar. Radar can be used to aim a gun or missile at a target, or to detect missiles that are entering the area covered by the radar. Ships and planes carry radar to show them their own position and the position of other craft nearby. It is also used in police work and in scientific research. The police use radar to measure the speed of vehicles in order to control speeding on the highways. Radar

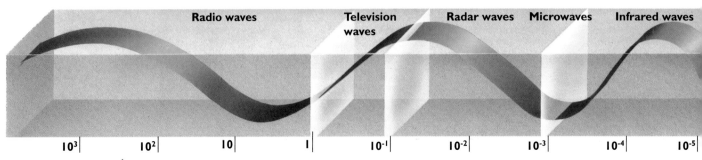

| | Radio waves | Television waves | Radar waves | Microwaves | Infrared waves |

10^3 10^2 10 1 10^{-1} 10^{-2} 10^{-3} 10^{-4} 10^{-5}

waves have been bounced off Venus and Mars to help scientists study and map those planets.

▶ ▶ ▶ ▶ **FIND OUT MORE** ◀ ◀ ◀ ◀
Air Traffic Control; Physics;
Radio; Radio Astronomy

☼ RADIATION

Sunlight, radio waves, and ripples on the surface of a body of water are all examples of radiation. Radiation is the way energy moves through substances or space.

Mechanical radiation is waves moving through matter—something that you can touch or feel, such as water or air. The matter the waves pass through is called the *medium*. The waves start when an object disturbs the medium. For instance, when a rock hits water it pushes *particles* (bits) of water out of the way. These particles move the particles next to them. In this way a wave moves across the water.

Waves of *electromagnetic* energy do not need a medium. Electromagnetic waves, such as light or radio waves, can travel through empty space. These waves are formed by the *oscillations* (vibrations) of electric and magnetic fields. Although they can travel through empty space, electromagnetic waves may change slightly when they pass through matter, or they may be *absorbed* (soaked up) by the matter. Electromagnetic waves travel through space at the speed of light, 186,000 miles (299,330 km) a second. The energy

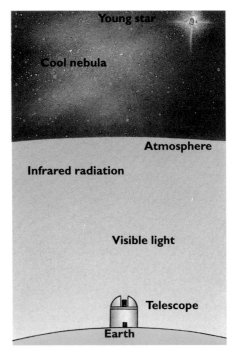

of a wave depends on its *wavelength* (distance between waves) and *frequency* (number of waves each second). The longer the wavelength, the lower the frequency. Electromagnetic waves can have wavelengths as long as several miles, or so short that millions of waves could fit across a pinhead. The longest electromagnetic waves are radio waves, the shortest are gamma rays. In between are microwaves, infrared rays, visible light, ultraviolet light, and X rays.

Nuclear radiation is given off by the *nucleus* of an atom. This type of radiation consists of electromagnetic energy and streams of small particles. If the nucleus is hit by another particle, it may split and release nuclear radiation.

We could not live without radiation—it is an important and vital part of our everyday lives. If electro-

◀ **Infrared radiation from distant objects in space can penetrate the Earth's atmosphere more easily than visible light, much of which is reflected. Astronomers use infrared photography to observe objects in space, because the human eye can see only visible light.**

▽ **The electromagnetic spectrum is made up of energy that moves in a wave motion at a fixed speed— that of light. The only difference between the various kinds of rays is their particular wavelength. Visible light, the only rays we can see, is at the center.**

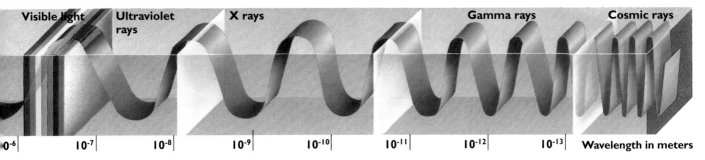

▶ **A microwave oven uses microwaves to heat food. Microwaves are electromagnetic waves that are reflected by metal, but can be absorbed by many other solid objects.**

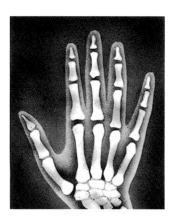

▲ **X rays can pass right through the body's soft tissues, so doctors use them to see the bones inside the body. Doses are always kept to a minimum, because X rays can be harmful to humans.**

magnetic waves could not travel through empty space, the light and heat from the sun would never reach Earth. If the light (energy) from the sun could not reach the Earth, there would be no life here. Without radiation we could not hear or see. Sounds travel to our ears in the form of mechanical radiation. All light travels as electromagnetic waves.

▶▶▶▶ **FIND OUT MORE** ◀◀◀◀
Electricity; Nuclear Energy; Radioactivity; Sound; Spectrum; Wave; X Rays

 RADIATION BELT

Two distinct *radiation belts*, zones of electrically charged particles, circle the Earth like huge doughnuts. Dr. James Van Allen discovered the belts in 1958, from information collected by the first American satellite, *Explorer I*.

The inner belt begins about 400 miles (650 km) above the Earth's surface and extends outward to about 4,000 miles (6,500 km). This belt is thickest at the equator and thinnest at the poles. The outer belt begins about 8,000 miles (13,000 km) above the Earth and extends outward to about 12,000 miles (20,000 km).

The particles in the belts are held in place by the same force that pulls a compass needle toward north—the magnetic field of the Earth. Charged particles given off by the sun stream toward the Earth in a *solar wind*. When they hit the Earth's magnetic field, they are trapped and bounce back and forth inside the field, from north to south. Other particles, coming from outer space or from the Earth's atmosphere, may be trapped in the same way.

Excessive radiation can make human beings and other animals sick and can damage electronic equipment. Spacecraft must pass through the belts quickly or have heavy shielding to block the radiation.

Other planets with strong magnetic fields, such as Jupiter, also have radiation belts.

▶▶▶▶ **FIND OUT MORE** ◀◀◀◀
Radiation; Space Travel

▶ **The Earth's environment is dominated by its magnetic field. Protons and electrons sent out by the sun in the solar wind become entangled in the field. The densest regions of trapped particles are two Van Allen belts. The solar wind has deformed the outer magnetic field into an egg shape.**

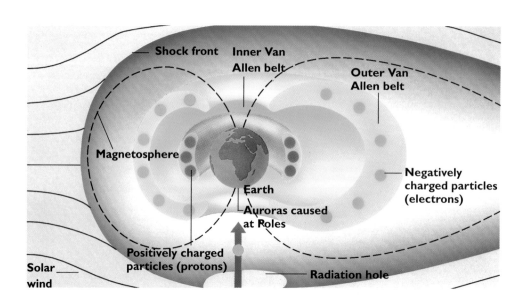

Shock front — Inner Van Allen belt — Outer Van Allen belt — Magnetosphere — Negatively charged particles (electrons) — Earth — Auroras caused at Poles — Positively charged particles (protons) — Solar wind — Radiation hole

RADIO

The sounds you listen to on a radio have had a very complicated journey. Suppose you are listening to an announcer reading the news over a radio. The announcer is sitting in a broadcasting studio miles from your home. The announcer speaks into a microphone. Inside the microphone is a thin sheet of metal. Each sound that strikes the sheet of metal makes it *vibrate*, or shake back and forth very quickly. The metal vibrates a different way for each different sound that strikes it.

The microphone changes all of these vibrations into very weak electrical signals, called *audio signals*. Each different kind of vibration produces a different audio signal. The microphone is connected to a radio transmitter by an electric wire. Inside the radio transmitter is equipment that makes the audio signals stronger.

The transmitter also makes a much higher frequency electrical signal called a *carrier signal*. The radio transmitter then adds the audio signals to the carrier signal. Adding the audio signal to the carrier is called *modulating* the carrier. The modulation can be either *amplitude* modulation (AM radio) or *frequency* modulation (FM radio). In amplitude modulation, adding the audio signal changes the height of the carrier signal. In frequency modulation, the audio signal changes the instant of time between carrier signals. Finally, the radio transmitter sends the modulated carrier signal to a large radio antenna. As the modulated carrier travels through the antenna, it gives off radio waves. The radio waves move out in all directions at the speed of light, 186,000 miles (300,000 km) a second.

A carrier signal and the carrier wave it produces vibrate thousands of times every second. You can compare a carrier signal with a whistle.

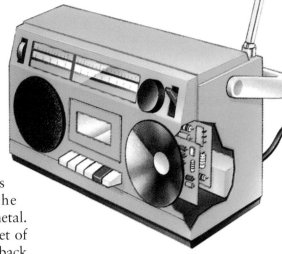

Most radios have the same basic design, though they come in a wide range of sizes. Radios are powered by electricity, either from batteries or from a plug and socket. The tuner on the front selects the radio stations.

The whistling sound is also made up of vibrations. These vibrations travel through the air. Now, if you made a steady whistling noise that did not change at all, this noise would be like the carrier signal that a radio transmitter makes. Start to whistle a tune now. In a way, you have added the tune to the whistling sound. Something like this happens inside the radio transmitter when the announcer's voice is added to the carrier signal. The carrier signal with the announcer's voice added to it is sent into the air as radio waves to be picked up by the receiving antenna.

Inside Your Radio

When radio waves strike the antenna of your radio, the antenna turns the waves back into weak electrical signals before they travel into the radio.

The radio makes these weak electrical signals stronger, and separates the carrier signal from the audio signals that carry the sounds made by the announcer. Finally, the radio sends these audio signals to a loudspeaker. The signals make the loudspeaker vibrate in the same way as the thin piece of metal in the microphone. These vibrations leave the loudspeaker and travel through the air, where you hear them as sounds.

You can listen to many different radio stations on the radio. You pick a station by turning or pushing a knob. This is called "tuning"—choosing one carrier over another.

Radio waves can be as much as 10 miles (16 km) long. The waves given out by red light are only about .00003 of an inch (.000075 cm) long; the waves of violet light are only half the length of red waves. Other electromagnetic waves such as X rays and ultraviolet rays are much shorter still. Because these waves have such tiny lengths, scientists use a convenient unit when talking about them. This unit is the ångström. An ångström is one hundred millionth of a centimeter. The wavelength of red light is therefore about 7,500 ångström.

The first radio broadcast to contain speech and music was made on December 24, 1906, in the United States. The broadcast was given by the Canadian inventor Reginald Fessenden, who talked, sang, and played the violin. The first radio station began operating in New York in 1907.

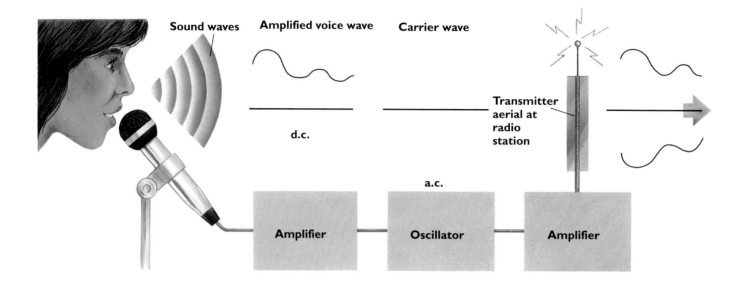

Sound waves | Amplified voice wave | Carrier wave

d.c.

a.c.

Amplifier | Oscillator | Amplifier

Transmitter aerial at radio station

▲ How a voice signal is transmitted and received by radio. The amplified signal from a microphone is made to *modulate* (vary) the *amplitude* (the height and depth) of a carrier wave continuously transmitted at the radio station. The signal is picked up by the receiver aerial, then amplified and demodulated to recreate the original voice signal. This is known as amplitude modulation (AM). An alternative technique is frequency modulation (FM), where the voice signal is made to modulate the frequency of the carrier wave.

When radio was first invented, the people who wanted to build radio transmitters used whatever carrier signals they wanted to. If two people used the same carrier signal, their radio signals got mixed up. If you tried to tune your radio to one of these stations, you would hear the other station also. It is the same as if two people tried to whistle two different songs at the same time. Other people would find it hard to distinguish between the songs.

To prevent this kind of confusion, the U.S. government established the Federal Communications Commission, or FCC. The FCC told every radio station what carrier signal it could use. Now the radio stations cannot interfere with each other.

Each station's carrier signal has a different *wavelength* (distance between waves). This means that it has a different *frequency* (number of waves each second). AM stations transmit long wavelengths at low frequencies. FM stations transmit shorter wavelengths at higher frequencies. "Short-wave" stations transmit wavelengths shorter than AM but longer than FM. Short waves can be broadcast for thousands of miles, so they are used for long-range communications and international broadcasting. Radio amateurs send short-wave messages all over the world.

▶▶▶▶ **FIND OUT MORE** ◀◀◀◀
Electricity; Radiation; Radio Broadcasting; Sound; Spectrum; Television; Wave

▶ A simple radio. The radio signals are passed from the aerial to the tuning circuit via the coil. The coil and the capacitor can be tuned to the radio station selected. The diode produces audio frequency current for the earpiece.

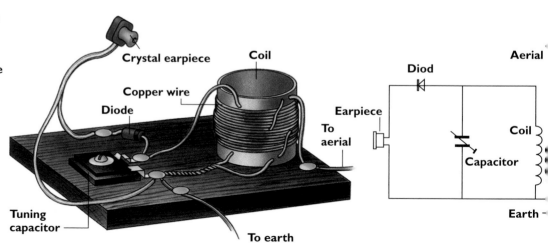

Crystal earpiece | Coil | Aerial
Copper wire | Diod
Diode | Earpiece
To aerial | Coil
Capacitor
Tuning capacitor
To earth
Earth

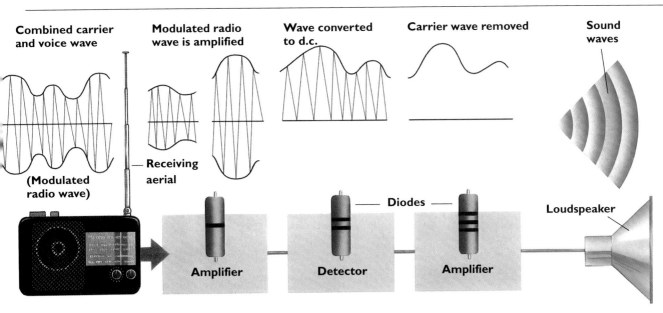

Combined carrier and voice wave — (Modulated radio wave) — Receiving aerial

Modulated radio wave is amplified

Wave converted to d.c.

Carrier wave removed

Sound waves

Diodes

Loudspeaker

Amplifier — Detector — Amplifier

RADIO AMATEUR

Have you ever listened to faraway stations on a shortwave radio? Radio amateurs, or "hams," can both listen and talk to stations all over the world.

A ham radio station has a *transmitter*, for sending radio signals; a *receiver*, for receiving signals; and an *antenna*. Some hams build their own stations from kits, while others buy their equipment ready-made. A complete radio ham station can be small enough to fit on a desk, or large enough to fill a room.

Amateur radio is the only hobby that is regulated by national and international law. In order to become a ham, you must first get a license from the government. Most hams begin with a *novice* license. To get this license you have to pass a simple test. Novices can use only Morse code on their stations. Children as young as 6 have received licenses. The next step is either a *technician class* license or a *general class* license. These allow you to talk with other hams. Experienced amateurs can obtain more advanced licenses.

In 1958, the U.S. government set aside certain radio frequencies as the *Citizens Band*. This band has become very popular with emergency personnel, truck drivers, and many others who use it for business, for reporting emergencies, and just for conversation. No technical knowledge is required to use a "CB" radio, and the operator needs no license though his or her radio does. CB operators have a colorful language of their own, and listening to them can be very amusing. *Transceivers* (transmitters and receivers) are sold in many stores. License applications come with them for the new owner's convenience.

▶▶▶▶ **FIND OUT MORE** ◀◀◀◀
Morse Code;
Radio; Radio Broadcasting

▼ An amateur radio "ham" at work. To be able to use amateur radio, you must first pass a test to get a license. There are various types of licenses that a ham can get, depending on his or her level of experience.

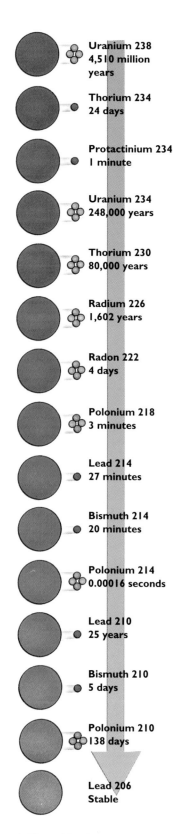

Uranium 238	4,510 million years
Thorium 234	24 days
Protactinium 234	1 minute
Uranium 234	248,000 years
Thorium 230	80,000 years
Radium 226	1,602 years
Radon 222	4 days
Polonium 218	3 minutes
Lead 214	27 minutes
Bismuth 214	20 minutes
Polonium 214	0.00016 seconds
Lead 210	25 years
Bismuth 210	5 days
Polonium 210	138 days
Lead 206	Stable

▲ The table above shows the radioactive series that begins with uranium 238 and ends with lead. The time given is the half-life of each element.

☼ RADIOACTIVITY

All elements are made up of *atoms*. Millions of atoms could make up the dot of this "i." Every atom has a *nucleus*—a small, hard inner core—and *electrons*— negative electrical charges that circle the nucleus the way the moon circles the Earth.

A nucleus is not all one piece. It is made up of *protons*—heavy particles with positive electrical charges—and *neutrons*—heavy particles with no electrical charge. The number of protons in an atom determines what element it is. An element is radioactive if its nucleus is *unstable*—tending to decay, or break apart.

Radium is a radioactive metal found in uranium ore. When a radium atom decays, it gives off an *alpha particle*—a bundle of two protons and two neutrons. Because it has lost two protons, the atom is no longer an atom of radium. It is now an atom of another element, called *radon*. Radon is radioactive, too. The radon atom eventually gives off an alpha particle and becomes a polonium atom.

Radium, radon, and polonium are just three steps in a long chain of radioactive decay, starting with uranium and ending with lead, which is not radioactive. Not all of the radioactive elements give off alpha particles. Some of them give off *beta* particles—electrons made in the nucleus. The emission of alpha and beta particles is often accompanied by the emission of *gamma rays*.

⬤ Alpha particle

⬤ Beta particle

〜 Gamma ray

▼ Exposure, especially over long periods, to radioactive material may be very harmful. This radiation sign is used to warn people of the presence of radioactivity in the vicinity.

Gamma rays are electromagnetic waves. They act like *quanta* (bundles) of energy that fly through space at the speed of light.

The energy given off by a decaying nucleus is tremendous, considering the small size of the atom. The radioactive decay of one ounce (28 g) of uranium gives off as much energy as the burning of 50,000 pounds (22,680 kg) of coal. A radioactive element can be made to decay all at once, as in a nuclear bomb, but in nature only a few atoms decay at a time. The rate of decay of an element is called the element's *half-life*—the amount of time it takes for half of the atoms to decay. The half-life of most natural uranium is 4½ billion years. What was an ounce (28 g) of uranium 4½ billion years ago is now only half an ounce (14 g). The other half

▼ There are three forms of radioactivity—alpha, beta, and gamma radiation. Each type of radiation has a different penetrating ability. These different abilities are illustrated in the diagram shown below.

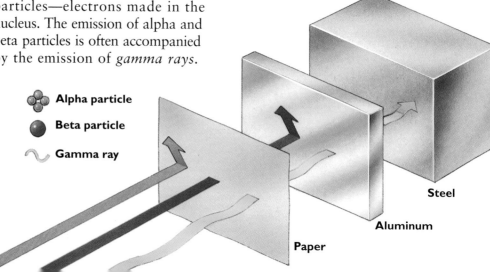

Steel

Aluminum

Paper

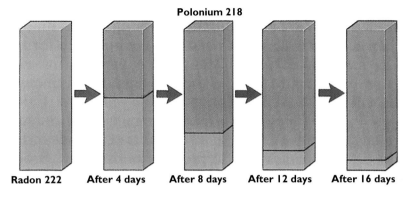

Polonium 218

Radon 222   After 4 days   After 8 days   After 12 days   After 16 days

▶ The element radon 222 has a half-life of approximately four days. As this element decays, it changes into polonium 218. The diagram shows the increasing proportion of polonium 218 over a period of 16 days.

ounce has decayed into other elements and energy. Not all radioactive elements have half-lives as long as uranium. Polonium 214 has a half-life of less than a millionth of a second.

The half-lives of radioactive substances can be useful in *dating* (finding out the age of) things. All *organisms* (living things) contain carbon, some of which is in the form of radiocarbon (also known as carbon 14), a radioactive form of carbon that has the same number of protons but a different number of neutrons. Radiocarbon is made in our atmosphere by the action of sunlight on nitrogen. Once an organism dies, it takes in no more radiocarbon from the air. The radiocarbon it has starts to decay releasing beta particles as it returns to a stable form of nitrogen. By measuring the proportion of radiocarbon in the *fossils* (buried remains) of organisms, scientists can tell how long they have been dead.

Radioactivity was discovered in 1896 by the French scientist Antoine Henri Becquerel. Becquerel noticed that a piece of uranium could blacken a photographic plate, even when black paper was put between them. The blackening was caused by the radiation from the uranium. Radioactivity is measured in units called *becquerels,* named after him. Two other French scientists, Marie and Pierre Curie, gave this radiation the name "radioactivity," and discovered that radioactivity was a property of the uranium itself, and not the result of chemical action.

Radioactivity is a very useful but dangerous *phenomenon* (fact). Small doses of radioactivity can be used to cure diseases, but larger doses are poisonous. Controlled radioactivity

(nuclear energy) can provide the power to run ships, factories, and cities. Uncontrolled radioactivity has the power to destroy. The most serious accident so far in the field of nuclear energy occurred in April 1986 at the Chernobyl Power Plant in the Ukraine, then part of the former Soviet Union. The core of the nuclear reactor overheated when the cooling system failed, and an explosion released a cloud of radiation that spread far from the plant. Radioactivity levels rose in many European countries. By May, 23 people had died as a result of the disaster. The long-term effects of the high radioactivity were unknown then, and are still unknown today.

▶ ▶ ▶ ▶ **FIND OUT MORE** ◀ ◀ ◀ ◀
Atom; Curie Family;
Element; Fallout; Geiger Counter;
Nuclear Energy; Radiation

▼ **Antoine Henri Becquerel, the French physicist who discovered radioactivity in 1896. For his work, he shared the 1903 Nobel Prize in physics with Marie and Pierre Curie.**

The alpha particles given off by radioactive substances are not a great danger to people, because they are stopped by the outer layer of the skin. Beta particles are more penetrating and can get inside the skin. Gamma rays are like very strong X rays and can easily penetrate matter. They pass right through the human body and can cause harm to the atoms inside.

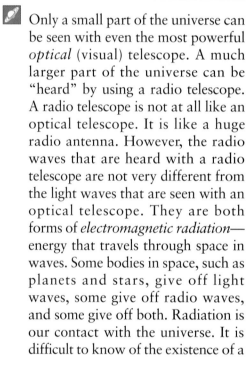

▲ The world's largest fully steerable radio telescope, at Effelsberg, Germany, has a reflecting dish 328 feet (100 m) across. It receives radio emissions from objects ranging from the whispering cool clouds of hydrogen in our own galaxy to the strident quasars that seem to signal from the edge of the universe.

▼ A radio telescope picks up the radio signals from a star.

RADIO ASTRONOMY

Only a small part of the universe can be seen with even the most powerful *optical* (visual) telescope. A much larger part of the universe can be "heard" by using a radio telescope. A radio telescope is not at all like an optical telescope. It is like a huge radio antenna. However, the radio waves that are heard with a radio telescope are not very different from the light waves that are seen with an optical telescope. They are both forms of *electromagnetic radiation*— energy that travels through space in waves. Some bodies in space, such as planets and stars, give off light waves, some give off radio waves, and some give off both. Radiation is our contact with the universe. It is difficult to know of the existence of a body that does not give off radiation.

Different substances give off different kinds of radiation. Hydrogen, the most common element in the universe, gives off radio waves with a wavelength of 8¼ inches (21 centimeters). When a radio telescope picks up wave length of 8¼ inches, the astronomers suspect that hydrogen is present. Radio astronomy has helped astronomers to construct a map of the hydrogen in our galaxy. Radio waves can also tell astronomers how hot the surface of an object is. Different temperatures have different wave lengths.

If a body gives off more radio waves than light, an astronomer can learn more about its makeup by listening to it than by looking at it. *Quasars* (*quasi*-stellar radio sources) give off little light but very strong radio waves. Their waves show a *shift* (change) in wavelength that suggests that some are moving away at 150,000 miles (241,000 km) a second. We are still not sure what quasars are, but they may be galaxies at the far edge of the known universe.

The antenna of a radio telescope looks like a huge dish or the blade of a snow shovel. The antenna picks up the radio waves and a *radiometer* measures their *intensity* (strength). Radio waves from space can have wavelengths of less than an inch (2.5 cm) or more than 50 feet (15 m). To catch the larger waves, several antennas are put side by side in a long row. A radio telescope with several antennas is called an *interferometer*. Some are more than a mile (1.6 km) long and are often cross-shaped. Interferometers help astronomers locate wave sources. Information from interferometers thousands of miles apart may be compared.

Radio waves from space were first detected by the American astronomer Karl Jansky in 1932. Shortly afterward, one of Jansky's students, Grote Reber, built the first radio telescope. It had a 31-foot-wide

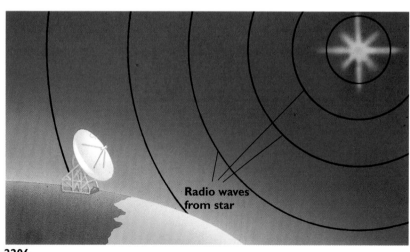

Radio waves from star

(9.5-m-wide) dish-shaped antenna. Today, the largest dish-shaped radio telescope, dug out of limestone in Arecibo, Puerto Rico, is 1,000 feet (305 m) across. The largest radio telescope of any kind was completed in 1981 at Socorro, New Mexico. This telescope is Y-shaped with each arm 13 miles (21 km) long with 27 mobile antennas on rails.

▶▶▶▶ **FIND OUT MORE** ◀◀◀◀
Astronomy; Observatory; Radio; Radiation; Star

⚙ RADIO BROADCASTING

In 1922, there were only 600 radio broadcasting stations in operation in the United States. Today, the number has increased to more than 10,000.

Radio broadcasting is a way of communicating to a large audience by sending radio programs over the air. Communication devices that reach very large audiences are called *mass media*. Radio broadcasting is one of the mass media. By combining voices, music, and sound effects, radio broadcasters have developed ways of broadcasting news, sports events, drama, music, and advertisements. Because you cannot see a picture on radio, broadcasters try to arouse the listeners' imaginations and get them to picture things.

Among the pioneers in radio development were Heinrich Hertz, a German physicist; Guglielmo Marconi, an Italian electrical engineer; and Lee De Forest, an American inventor. Hertz's experiments with electromagnetic waves led to the development of wireless radio. Marconi obtained his first patent on wireless telegraphy in 1896, and achieved communication across the English Channel two years later. De Forest designed a number of transmitters and, in 1916, reported the results of the Presidential election in the first radio news broadcast in the United States.

▲ A scene in a radio studio in the 1940s. The soundproof control booth is at the rear.

Radio Entertainment

From the 1920s to 1950s, radio stations offered a wide range of programs—variety shows, radio drama, mysteries, soap operas, westerns, and comedy shows. Television has taken over most of these types of programs, and radio is now pretty much limited to news, music, and special broadcasts (such as sports events, operas, and call-in talk shows). Radio programs are still very popular, however. About 85 percent of all Americans listen to radio at least once a day. People listen to radio as they drive their cars. Many people take portable transistor radios on picnics or to the beach. Sometimes you can hear radio broadcasts piped over speakers in stores, and office buildings. And, of course, many people listen to radio in their homes, especially for music and news.

On Sunday mornings, local radio stations broadcast church services and religious discussion programs, as well as news and music. Some stations broadcast only news, classical or popular music, educational shows, or foreign language programs.

Radio Frequency

All radio stations that broadcast in the United States must be licensed by the Federal Communications Commission (FCC). By granting a license, the FCC permits the station to use a particular airwave frequency. According to law, all U.S. airwaves

In November 1915, the human voice was heard across the Atlantic for the first time. It was a transmission from the U.S. Navy station at Arlington, Virginia, to the Eiffel Tower in Paris, France. The longest continuous radio broadcast was the reading of James Joyce's *Ulysses* on Radio Telefiss Eireann on July 16 and 17, 1982. It lasted 29 hours, 38 minutes, 47 seconds.

▲ Radio broadcasts are made from sound studios, like the one pictured here. The announcer works in a soundproof room. A technician monitors the "sounds" of the broadcasts and corrects any distortions on the sound-mixing desk (in the foreground).

▲ In Australia, children who live a long way from the nearest school often join the School of the Air. This is a school where children do not see their teachers, but talk to them over the radio instead.

are owned by the people. The government simply gives permission for broadcasters to use them. The FCC license must be renewed every three years. If a station broadcasts programs that are in some way harmful to people, the broadcaster's license is taken away. The National Association of Radio and Television Broadcasters (an organization of licensed station owners) has set up rules about the kinds of programs appropriate for broadcasting.

You can tune in to two types of radio stations—AM (amplitude modulation) or FM (frequency modulation). The initials AM and FM indicate the type of airwave over which a station broadcasts. AM radio waves vary in length at low frequencies. FM radio is carried by shorter waves at higher frequencies.

Radio Industry

In the United States, broadcasting is a business in which station owners try to make a profit. Station owners sell

air time (broadcast time) to businesses that use the time to advertise their products. Stations also get advertisers to *sponsor* (pay the cost of) shows in exchange for radio advertising time.

In some nations, such as the former Soviet Union, Poland, and Denmark, all radio and television stations are owned and run by the government. Government-owned stations do not need advertising. Nations such as Great Britain have stations that are not run by the government directly. The British government has licensed a *public service company* called the British Broadcasting Corporation (BBC). The cost of programs is paid for by setting up a tax on all radio and television sets. The government gives these tax revenues to the BBC, and the corporation provides radio and television programs with the money.

A radio *network* is a combination of widely spaced stations that agree to carry the same programs in exchange for fees paid by advertisers whose commercials are broadcast over the network. Belonging to a network saves local stations from having to create shows and get advertisers for every program they broadcast. Radio stations do not need to belong to networks, because they can often support themselves with money from local advertisers.

If you would like to work in radio broadcasting someday, there are many different types of jobs you could do. Radio *announcers* report the news, work as disc jockeys, give play-by-play descriptions of sports events, and often broadcast commercials. *Producers* decide which radio programs to broadcast. They locate sponsors and hire the announcers, interviewers, and other broadcast talent. Radio *directors* actually direct the progress of a radio broadcast. Radio *engineers* operate the equipment that sends broadcasts out over the air waves. *Writers* create scripts for radio shows, such as news broadcasts. Writers are also employed by advertisers to write commercial messages for broadcast on the air. Radio stations also have *librarians*. A librarian keeps track of the station's large collection of records, compact discs, and tape-recorded material.

You might like to visit a radio station to see an actual broadcast in operation. The announcer sits in a soundproof room and speaks through a microphone. The engineer *monitors* (listens to) the broadcast as it goes out to correct any distortion in sound or to add special electronic effects to the sound when needed. The director gives the announcer cues about when to begin speaking, or when a commercial or station break must be announced. Directors and announcers must make sure there is no *dead air time* (long pauses without any sound coming over the air). If the station has dead spots in its broadcasts, people tuning in will not realize that the station is on the air. This is why announcers keep talking, no matter what. Good announcers must be able to talk about anything on the spur of the moment to keep the airwaves alive.

▶ ▶ ▶ ▶ **FIND OUT MORE** ◀ ◀ ◀ ◀
Communication; Radio; Radio Amateur; Television; Television Broadcasting

☼ RADIOCARBON DATING

In the summer of 1991, hikers in the Italian Alps found the body of a prehistoric man on a glacier. The skin, hair, and leather clothing of the "ice man" had been perfectly preserved.

European people at the time the "ice man" lived could not read or write, so scientists could not examine any writing or coins to tell how old he was. Instead, they used a technique called *radiocarbon dating*.

Radiocarbon dating is a method of determining the age of objects that were once alive. These objects can be either plants or animals.

Radiocarbon is a radioactive form of carbon. It is formed when cosmic rays strike atoms in the earth's atmosphere, releasing protons, neutrons, and electrons. Some of these particles turn nitrogen atoms into radiocarbon.

Much of the carbon in the atmosphere is in the form of carbon dioxide gas. A tiny amount of this gas contains some radiocarbon, but even that small amount can be detected. Plants absorb radiocarbon in the carbon dioxide that they need for growth. Animals then absorb radiocarbon by eating plants.

Radiocarbon has a half-life of about 5,730 years. That means that a once-living object loses half of its

▼ **Radiocarbon begins to decay at a constant rate as soon as a plant or animal dies. After 70,000 years, it will have decayed almost completely.**

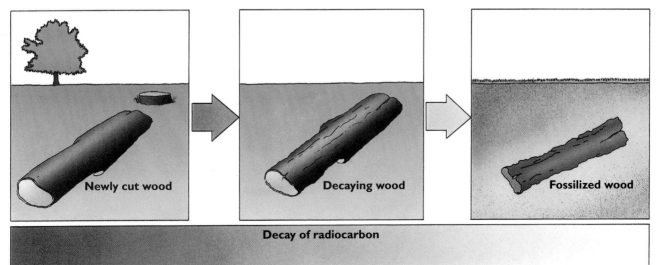

Newly cut wood   Decaying wood   Fossilized wood

Decay of radiocarbon

carbon radioactivity after 5,730 years. Half of this remaining amount is lost after the next 5,730 years, and so on.

Scientists need only a very small piece of an object for radiocarbon dating. They can burn the piece and examine the result with a radiation counter, or they can use particle accelerators to measure the radiation without burning the sample.

Radiocarbon dating is an important tool for archaeologists and geologists. It gives an accurate picture of life up to 50,000 years ago. Sometimes it can also lead to surprises. The "ice man" used a type of spear that was common in the Bronze Age. Radiocarbon dating showed that he had died hundreds of years before the Bronze Age began in 3500 B.C.!

▶▶▶ **FIND OUT MORE** ◀◀◀
Alps; Bronze and Bronze Age;
Prehistory; Radioactivity

⚙ RAILROAD

Before the invention of the automobile and the airplane, railroads were the fastest and most widely used method of carrying mail, food, fuel, other freight, and passengers from place to place. Today, railroads are still a major means of freight shipment, but they are not the "kings" of transportation they once were. A railroad is really a transportation network, rather than simply a vehicle for transportation. A great deal of equipment, thousands of workers, and miles of tracks and railroad cars go into making a railroad.

Certain railroad employees work aboard a train. The *engineer* runs the locomotive. The fireman assists the engineer. The *conductor* is in charge of all of the train except the locomotive.

Brakemen assist the conductor. *Porters* wait on passengers in Pullman cars. But many other people off the train are needed to keep a railroad running. A *repair crew* keeps cars and locomotives in running condition. *Dispatchers* determine the routes trains will follow and signal the engineers on trains. *Station employees* sell tickets and load freight and baggage.

Classification Yards
Trains are made up in *classification yards*, where the necessary cars are coupled together and attached to locomotives. In automatically controlled classification yards, cars are switched with electric "eyes," which pick up codes on the cars and route

The first passenger train in America made its initial trip from Charleston, South Carolina, to Hamburg, South Carolina, in 1830. The newspaper account of the trip read: "The passengers flew on wings of the wind...at the fantastic speed of 15 miles an hour."

▼ An electric locomotive. It picks up electricity from power lines overhead or beside the track and this is fed via motor control circuits to the drive motors that drive the wheels.

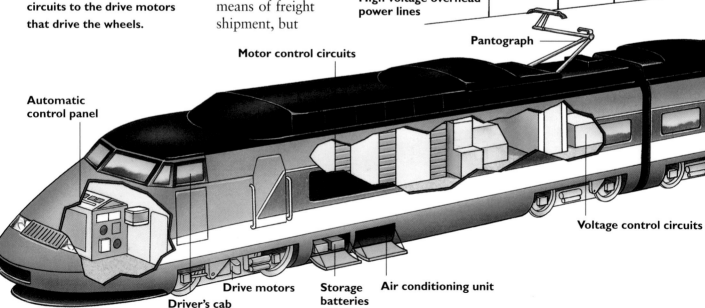

High voltage overhead power lines

Pantograph

Motor control circuits

Automatic control panel

Voltage control circuits

Drive motors

Driver's cab

Storage batteries

Air conditioning unit

them to the proper track. The *rolling stock* (cars and locomotives) is cleaned, repaired, and refueled in other yards.

Signals and Controls

Railroads have complicated systems of automatic and manual signals that control the routing, braking, and, in some cases, even the speed of trains on their tracks. The dispatchers are railroad employees who control all train routes. They control the electric light signals that appear over the tracks and, in some cases, in the locomotive cabs. These lights either form lines set in different ways or show different colors, signaling the locomotive driver to stop, heed caution, or go.

The Centralized Traffic Control system (CTC) is a modern way of handling railroad communication. Under this system, the position of the trains is shown continuously on an electric diagram in front of the dispatcher, who sends signals to engineers, using special equipment in the control tower. The CTC system also uses radio for communication between the dispatcher and engineer. Microwave communication is one of the newest developments in the railroad industry. Microwave messages are sent from the control tower to saucer-shaped receivers on pedestals above the train track. These receivers then send the messages (received in the form of flashing lights in the locomotive cab) to passing trains.

Some short-distance, or commuter, railroads operate under a system of automatic train control. In this system, an electric master control is located in the front of the locomotive just above the rails. The master control picks up electric current in the rails and interprets the kind of electric signal it has received. Then the master control tells the engineer what should be done by braking, flashing lights, or sounding bells. The master control also determines how fast the train can be operated.

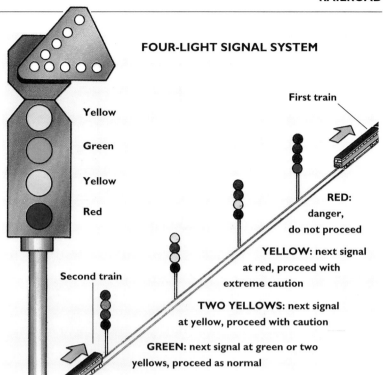

FOUR-LIGHT SIGNAL SYSTEM

Yellow
Green
Yellow
Red

Second train

First train

RED: danger, do not proceed

YELLOW: next signal at red, proceed with extreme caution

TWO YELLOWS: next signal at yellow, proceed with caution

GREEN: next signal at green or two yellows, proceed as normal

Types of Cars and Locomotives

FREIGHT CARS. The railroad industry makes most of its money from shipping freight. There are *freight cars* to carry almost anything. *Boxcars* are closed cars used to ship material that simply needs protection from weather and loss. *Flatcars* consist of a floor attached to the wheels, without sides or top. Flatcars are used for carrying heavy, wide loads, such as logs, that will not be harmed by exposure to the weather. *Tank cars* are cylindrical-shaped, closed cars built for carrying liquids, such as oil or chemicals. *Refrigerator cars* carry food products that would spoil in ordinary boxcars. *Hoppers,* either open-top or closed, are funnel-shaped cars that carry materials such as coal, grain, or gravel. *Auto-rack cars* contain either two or three racks for transporting automobiles. *Piggy-back* cars carry the trailer (but not the cab) of a large truck. Goods can be shipped rapidly over long distances by piggy-back. At the railroad station nearest the destination, the trailer is attached to a truck cab. The rest of the trip is then made by truck. This method of shipment is known as "Tructrain service." A *unit train* is made up of cars carrying the same

▲ Railway signals tell the train driver whether the line ahead is clear or not. This is a four-light signal system. It allows plenty of time for the driver to stop the train if he needs to do so.

▲ One of many freight trains that carry cargo through the United States.

▲ Railway locomotives and wagons have solid wheels. The projecting wheel rims fit over the T-shaped rails, so that the train can run along the top of the rails without falling off.

▼ Different types of locomotives drawn up at a station. It is very unlikely that you would see all of them together in one place, although all types, even steam locomotives, are still in use.

product. Unit trains often save a railroad time and money. The *caboose,* the last car in a freight train, contains sleeping quarters and a kitchen for the train crew. A caboose is seldom used today.

PASSENGER SERVICE. The two main types of passenger trains in operation today are *commuter trains* and *intercity trains.* Commuter trains (between a city and its suburbs) carry millions of people to and from work in such cities as New York, Chicago, Tokyo, Paris, and London. This is often referred to as *rapid transit.* Intercity trains (for example, from New York to Washington, D.C.) travel at a high speed and make longer runs than commuter trains do. Fast intercity trains serve cities in Japan, France, Canada, the United States, and other countries. These trains may have *sleeping,* or *Pullman, cars* for long trips and *dining cars. Club cars* or *observation cars* are cars where passengers can go to get some food and drink, relax, or look at the scenery. Some observation cars have windows around one end of the car

and a higher viewing deck to give passengers a better view.

LOCOMOTIVES. The locomotive consists of the engine and a cab for the engineer. The locomotive is mounted on wheels like other cars and provides the power that moves an entire train. The earliest locomotives, *steam locomotives,* were powered by steam engines. *Diesel locomotives,* first used in the 1920s and still in use, are more efficient than steam locomotives in converting fuel to mechanical energy, and diesels do not require so many fuel stops. *Electric locomotives* are cleaner and more efficient than diesels are. But electric locomotives need to obtain electric current from wires suspended above the track or from an electrified third rail. *Diesel-electric locomotives* run on electricity produced by their own oil-burning diesel engines. These locomotives are the most widely used in the United States today. Other types of locomotives include *gas-turbine electric locomotives* and *diesel-hydraulic locomotives.*

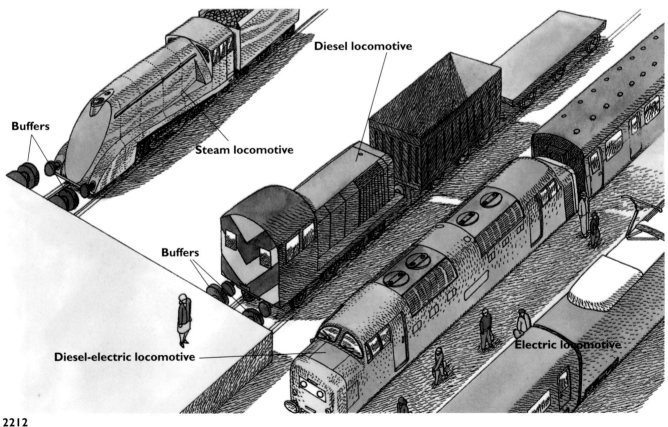

Buffers

Diesel locomotive

Steam locomotive

Buffers

Diesel-electric locomotive

Electric locomotive

Early Railroads

The earliest railroads were wagon ways built in mines in the 1500s and 1600s to haul out coal, ore, or stone. These railroads consisted of horse-drawn wagons traveling over wooden rails. *Crossties* (wooden beams or ties) were introduced to hold the rails in place, and the wooden tracks were soon replaced with iron ones. But horses, donkeys, or mules supplied the power until the beginning of the 1800s, when steam locomotives first came into use. The first practical locomotive was built in 1804 by the English engineer Richard Trevithick. Another Englishman, George Stephenson, improved the locomotive by returning the steam that escaped back into the engine. This increased the steam pressure in the engine, making it more powerful. Future steam locomotives were built according to Stephenson's example.

Commercial railroading began with the opening of the Stockton-Darlington Line in England in 1825.

◀ The original locomotive built in 1804 by the English engineer Richard Trevithick. Powered by steam, this was the locomotive that pioneered the railway age of the 1800s.

In 1830, the Charleston and Hamburg Railroad became the first American line to use steam locomotives. The Baltimore and Ohio (begun in 1830) began using steam locomotives the following year. France and Germany built railroads soon after, as did Russia, India, Australia, Africa, and other parts of the world. By 1900, one could cross North

▼ The steam locomotive uses coal as a fuel. The coal is burned in the firebox and heats the water in the locomotive's boiler. The water boils into steam, expanding from a liquid to a gas. This expansion provides the pressure that pushes the pistons that drive the wheels of the steam locomotive. However, steam is not a very efficient method of propulsion because too much fuel is wasted as heat.

Blastpipe   Safety valve   Boiler   Firebox

Piston

Connecting rods

Driving rod

Bogie truck

trial growth of the United States in the second half of the 1800s. People could go at least part of the way to newly settled territories by rail. When workers on the Central Pacific

▲ **The London and Midland Railway in England was the first all-steam railway to carry passengers on a regular schedule. The prototype locomotive for this railway was the "Rocket," designed by George Stephenson.**

▼ **Railroads played an important part on both sides during the Civil War. This Southern locomotive flies the Confederate flag.**

America or the former Soviet Union by train, or go from Paris, France, to Istanbul, Turkey.

When railroads first came into general use, railroad operators discovered some problems they had not anticipated. The *gauge* (width) between tracks varied from one railroad to another. This meant that the trains of one railroad could not run on the tracks of another railroad. The problem was solved by standardizing the gauge for all tracks. In the United States and many other countries, the standard gauge is 4 feet 8½ inches (1.4 m). In the United States, where tracks ran through wild, open country, an unlit track could be dangerous at night. At first, trains pushed ahead of them a flatcar of burning wood to provide light. Later, until electric lights came into use, a kerosene lamp with a reflector was attached to the front of the locomotive. Railroad operators had trouble with animals straying onto the track until the cowcatcher was invented. This was a frame attached to the lower front of the locomotive to clear the track ahead.

Railroads played a very important part in the rapid western expansion and indus-

▲ **One of the Union Pacific's "Big Boys," built in the early 1940s and considered to be the largest steam locomotive.**

and Union Pacific railroads met at Promontory Point, Utah, on May 10, 1869, they joined the rails of the two lines, creating a coast-to-coast railroad. Business and agriculture in new territories and states depended for survival upon rail shipment of their goods. Railroads also influenced the pattern of growth and settlement in the West. Towns were established near railroads, because people tended to settle there.

The federal government (and later, local governments) helped railroads grow by giving them grants of land on which to build tracks. But during the second half of the 1800s, railroad owners began dishonest and unfair practices in building, charging for freight, and competing with other railroads. The public had few defenses, because they needed railroads for transportation and freight shipment. But people began demand-

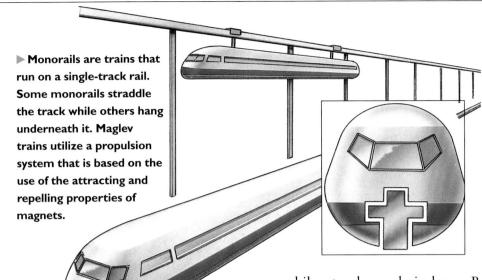

▶ **Monorails are trains that run on a single-track rail. Some monorails straddle the track while others hang underneath it. Maglev trains utilize a propulsion system that is based on the use of the attracting and repelling properties of magnets.**

QUIZ

1. What is *rolling stock?*
2. Which railroad employees control the routes trains take and the signals that appear over the tracks?
3. What is the name of the modern method of railroad communication?
4. What part of a train houses the engine?
5. When was the first coast-to-coast railroad completed in the U.S.?

(Answers on page 2304)

ing laws to restrict the railroad industry. In 1887, the Interstate Commerce Commission (ICC) was formed to regulate and control such railroad practices.

Railroads of the Future

Some kind of high-speed ground transportation is needed to relieve the heavy automobile traffic in cities and on highways. Railroads are working on this problem. A few countries, such as Japan and France, have already developed efficient, comfortable high-speed railroads. Engineers have been working for years on the *monorail,* a series of passenger-carrying vehicles (similar to railroad cars) riding on or suspended from an overhead rail. (A monorail runs several feet above the ground.) Monorails are still experimental, although one has been in operation in West Germany since 1901. Monorails have been used at several world's fairs and at amusement parks. If they prove practical, commercial monorails may be built in many places in the United States.

In the middle of this century, railroads began to lose a great deal of their business to newer and faster methods of transportation—auto-

mobiles, trucks, and airplanes. But with improved methods (such as the piggyback car) and more efficient service, railroads have won back some freight business, their major source of income.

Most U.S. passenger service now consists of commuter lines, serving the nation's major urban centers. At the same time, intercity passenger service is being reestablished. In 1971, a federal organization called Amtrak took over the operation of most U.S. intercity passenger trains. Federal government spending on railroads is still low compared to spending on highway construction and air and water transportation, but now, high-speed trains are being tested for interstate travel.

▶ ▶ ▶ ▶ **FIND OUT MORE** ◀ ◀ ◀ ◀
Subway; Transportation

RAIN AND SNOW

You know that rain and snow fall from clouds. Have you ever wondered how raindrops and snowflakes happen to be in clouds?

Clouds are made up of tiny droplets of water. The average droplet is only 34 millionths of an inch (0.0009 mm) in diameter. It is so light that it hangs in the air, moving downward very slowly. The air in a cloud is always moving around. This causes some of the droplets to

WHERE TO DISCOVER MORE

Coiley, John. *Train.* New York: Knopf, 1992.
Fisher, Leonard Everett. *Tracks Across America.* New York: Holiday House, 1992.

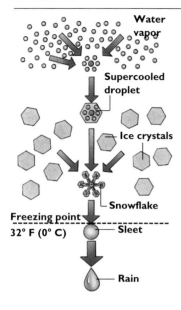

Water vapor

Supercooled droplet

Ice crystals

Snowflake

Freezing point
32° F (0° C)

Sleet

Rain

▲ Snowflakes are formed when the water vapor in clouds condenses. The droplets crystallize if the air is cold enough. The snowflakes become rain if they meet warmer air as they fall toward the ground.

▼ Each snowflake is different, but every one has six sides.

bump into others. The bumping droplets join together, forming larger droplets. The weight of a larger droplet enables it to overcome the movements of air. The droplet falls faster and faster. It bumps into more and more droplets and grows larger and larger.

Most rain clouds are very high from top to bottom. Before a falling droplet reaches the bottom of a cloud, it may be made up of a million tiny droplets and be one-twentieth of an inch (1.3 mm) in diameter. It has become a raindrop. It may grow to one-quarter of an inch. The joining of water droplets until they are heavy enough to fall is the way raindrops usually form in the tropics.

In the temperate regions of the Earth, the tops of rain clouds are cold enough for tiny ice crystals to form. The falling crystals pick up water droplets and other ice crystals. Snowflakes are formed. By the time the snowflakes reach the lower and warmer parts of the cloud, they melt and form raindrops.

If the temperature of a whole cloud is below freezing, and the temperature of the air on the ground is also below freezing, snow falls on the ground. Each snow crystal has a different lacy design and six sides or points.

The amount of rain, snow, sleet, hail, or other moisture that falls is called *precipitation*, a term often used by those who report the weather.

▶ ▶ ▶ ▶ **FIND OUT MORE** ◀ ◀ ◀ ◀
Cloud; Fog; Frost; Hail;
Humidity; Weather

RAINBOW

After a storm, tiny drops of water often remain in the air. When sunlight enters a water drop, it is *refracted*—bent and broken into colors. Then it is reflected off the inside of the drop, and when it leaves the drop, it is refracted again. The light is bent because light travels at a differ-

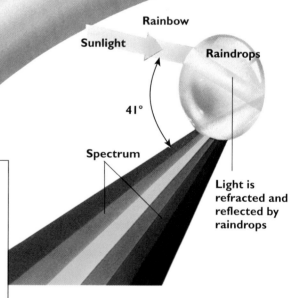

Rainbow

Sunlight

Raindrops

41°

Spectrum

Light is refracted and reflected by raindrops

▲ A rainbow is formed when sunlight is *refracted*, or bent, by raindrops. Each color in white light is bent in a slightly different way as it passes through the raindrop, so the light is split into the different colors of the spectrum—red, orange, yellow, green, blue, indigo, and violet.

LEARN BY DOING

It is easy to make a simple rain gauge. Take a glass jar, a plastic funnel with the same diameter as the jar, and a piece of stiff plastic. Bury the glass jar in the ground. Make a small hole in the piece of plastic, then put the spout of the funnel through the plastic. Place both funnel and plastic over the jar. When you remove the jar from the ground after it has rained, you will be able to measure the amount of rain that has fallen into the jar over a known period of time.

ent speed in water than it does in air. The light is broken into colors because different colors of light travel at different speeds in water.

After refraction, the different colors of light leave the drops at different angles, and appear at different angles in the sky. If you are looking in the direction of the drops, you will see bands of color arched across the sky, called a rainbow.

▶▶▶▶ **FIND OUT MORE** ◀◀◀◀
Color; Light; Spectrum

RAIN FOREST

SEE JUNGLE

RALEIGH, SIR WALTER (1552–1618)

Sir Walter Raleigh was an English adventurer, army commander, explorer, colonizer, and writer. He established one of the first colonies in North America, on Roanoke Island, North Carolina.

Raleigh began his career as a soldier. He fought with the Protestant Huguenots against the Catholics in France and for the British in Ireland. From 1578 to 1580, Raleigh and his half brother, Sir Humphrey Gilbert, went to sea to raid Spanish shipping in America.

Raleigh was a poet; he also wrote about travel and history. He became a favorite of Queen Elizabeth I, who made him a knight and commissioned him to seek new lands for England in the Americas. In 1585, Raleigh sent a group of about 100 men to Roanoke Island. The men did not develop farms or befriend the

LEARN BY DOING

You can make a rainbow yourself on a sunny day. Use a water hose with a spray nozzle. Stand with your back to the sun and spray the water away from you. You should be able to see a rainbow in the spray. What happens when you hold the hose at different angles? Or when you vary the spray?

Native Americans. When Sir Francis Drake passed by the next year, the men begged him to take them back to England.

Raleigh sent more colonists in 1587. When supply ships arrived to the settlement in 1591, there was no trace of them. To this day, the mystery of the "Lost Colony" has never been solved.

Raleigh's efforts to establish colonies in America brought England valuable information about the geography, native peoples, and plants of the New World. He introduced tobacco and potatoes to Europe.

WHERE TO DISCOVER MORE

Gallant, Roy A. *Rainbows, Mirages and Sundogs: The Sky As a Source of Wonder.* New York: Macmillan, 1987.

Taylor, Barbara. *Color and Light.* New York: Watts, 1990.

▶ **Queen Elizabeth I of England knighted Walter Raleigh in 1585. Raleigh's knighthood took place in the same year that he sent his first group of colonists to North America.**

Walter Raleigh spelled his name "Rawley" or "Rawleyghe" up to 1584. After that date, he always spelled it "Ralegh." He never spelled it Raleigh, as most people do today.

In 1595, Raleigh led an exploring trip to Guiana in South America. His ships went up the Orinoco River in what is now Venezuela. During the war with Spain in the 1590s, Raleigh's leadership as an admiral on the flagship, *Warspite*, helped the English capture the main Spanish seaport of Cadiz.

Raleigh was out of favor at court when King James came to the throne. The king wanted peace with Spain. In 1603, the king had Raleigh imprisoned for treason. In prison, Raleigh wrote a book called *History of the World*. After 13 years, he was released and allowed to search for gold in Guiana on the condition that he would not attack the Spanish. But his men fought with the Spanish and Raleigh's son, Wat, was killed. When Raleigh returned to England, the king ordered him beheaded for disobeying orders and attacking the Spanish. Fearless to the end, Raleigh joked with the executioner and gave the signal for the ax to fall.

▶ ▶ ▶ ▶ **FIND OUT MORE** ◀ ◀ ◀ ◀
Elizabeth I; Exploration

RANCHING

When settlers first moved westward into the Great Plains, they found vast areas of government-owned land known as the open range. It provided fine grazing for cattle and sheep. So cattle breeders set up large farms known as ranches. The great days of ranching were roughly between 1860 and 1890.

During that period, settlers were still moving westward, pushing back the frontier little by little. By 1890, the frontier had ceased to exist, and railroads had been built across the continent.

The men who herded the cattle on the range were known as *cowboys*. Each ranch had its own cattle, which were marked with a distinctive brand, such as the initials of the owner. When it came time to send the cattle to market, the cowboys from each ranch would ride out on the range to round up their own animals. Then the cattle would be driven to the nearest railroad depot. These cattle drives would often last as long as several weeks.

Cowboys' lives were rough and tough. They carried guns to fight off *rustlers* (cattle thieves). These guns were later used in bloody range wars when sheep farmers and *homesteaders* (small farmers) began competing for and fencing in the open land of the range.

Ranching still takes place today, but there is much less open range for cattle to graze. Cowboys, now generally called cowhands, still use horses for some of the rougher parts of the range, but they also use jeeps and trucks to get around. The bigger ranches often have their own helicopters. The raising of beef cattle is big business, and ranchers plant special grasses and use improved breeds of cattle to increase production.

▶ ▶ ▶ ▶ **FIND OUT MORE** ◀ ◀ ◀ ◀
Cattle; Cowboy; Great Plains

▼ **Hereford cattle on a ranch in the southwestern United States. In dry areas like this, cattle need a large acreage of land, so the ranches are very big.**

RANKIN, JEANNETTE (1880–1973)

The first woman to be elected to the U.S. Congress, and one of the most prominent campaigners for women's rights in the United States, was Jeannette Rankin. She was born on June 11, 1880, near Missoula, Montana. After attending college, she took up social work in Seattle, Washington, and became active in the struggle for women's *suffrage* (the right to vote and to hold public office).

In 1916, Jeannette Rankin was elected by Montana voters to the U.S. House of Representatives. She did not believe the United States should take part in World War I and spoke against it. This pacifist stance lost her the Republican Senate nomination in 1918. She ran as an independent but lost the election.

She returned to social work but was reelected to the House of Representatives in 1940. She voted against the U.S. declaration of war on Japan, and this virtually ended her career in politics. In the 1960s, she started a women's cooperative homestead in Georgia, and in 1968, at the age of 87, she led a women's protest against the Vietnam War.

▶ ▶ ▶ ▶ **FIND OUT MORE** ◀ ◀ ◀ ◀
Women's Rights

RAPHAEL (1483–1520)

One of the greatest painters of the Renaissance was Raphael (whose name in Italian is Raffaello Sanzio). Raphael was born in the northern Italian town of Urbino, where his father was the court painter for the Duke of Urbino. At the age of 21, Raphael went to Florence, where he studied the works of three great artists—Michelangelo, Leonardo da Vinci, and Fra Bartolommeo. He soon learned their techniques for showing light and shade, and for

painting dramatic action. Raphael showed an understanding of the structure of the human figure. Without copying their paintings, he was able to use their techniques in his own works. Learning to use others' ideas for his own purposes was one of Raphael's great talents.

At age 25, Raphael was called to Rome by Pope Julius II to paint frescoes in four small rooms of the Vatican. He did a variety of paintings there, one of which was *School of Athens*. (See the painting in the article on DIMENSION.) In this picture, you can see poses and gestures Raphael borrowed from Michelangelo's works. The architectural background and use of perspective are like those Leonardo da Vinci used in his painting of the *Last Supper*. But the result is Raphael's own work—a very great painting.

Raphael's job at the Vatican became much more important after he had been working there for a few years. Eventually, Raphael had 50 painters working for him, and later he was made chief architect of St. Peter's Basilica (church) at the Vatican.

Shown here is one of many paintings Raphael did of the Holy Family. If you study the way the picture is planned, you will see why Raphael is considered such a master of composition. The madonna is the center of attraction, yet the eyes of everyone in the painting are on the child, Jesus. St. John looks at Jesus from one side, and Joseph looks on from the other. The placement of Mary's arm moves your eyes up to Joseph to bring him in to the composition.

▶ ▶ ▶ ▶ **FIND OUT MORE** ◀ ◀ ◀ ◀
Leonardo da Vinci;
Michelangelo Buonarotti; Renaissance

RAPID TRANSIT SYSTEM

SEE RAILROAD, SUBWAY

▲ Jeannette Rankin, the first woman elected to the U.S. Congress.

▲ *The Holy Family*, by the Italian painter Raphael.

RARE ANIMAL

An animal may be rare because it is *endangered*—it is in danger of dying out—or because it is *ecologically restricted*—it can live only in a very few places. We usually say that an animal is endangered if its numbers are getting smaller—if more of the animals are dying than are being born, or if the animals are fewer now than they were in the past. Ecologically restricted animals are not always endangered, but they are always in danger of being so. If their homes are destroyed, they usually cannot go anywhere else. And since there are only a few of them, they can die out very quickly.

It is not unusual for an animal to die out or become *extinct*. Of all the animal *species* (kinds) that ever lived, only a tiny handful survives today. Often when a species died out in the past, a new and different species arose and took its place. The total number of species was not reduced, and the animal kingdom was as rich as before. But what is happening today is that species are dying out, and they

▲ The flightless Dodo. This bird, from the island of Mauritius in the Indian Ocean, was extinct by 1689.

▶ The last two great auks, birds of the Atlantic, were killed in 1844.

▲ A few European bison still survive on reserves in Poland.

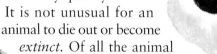

are all being replaced by only one species—human beings. A world with fewer animals is a poorer world for us.

Human beings kill other animals in two ways. The first way is simple killing—animals are slaughtered for their fur or meat, or because they are a nuisance, or just for fun. The second way a species is killed off is ecological destruction—destroying the places where animals live and the foods they eat, and disrupting the way they live. People also kill people, of course, and may soon find that they have endangered themselves.

Whales have been killed for their meat, for their oil, and for whalebone to make women's corsets. In the 1800s, millions of blue whales, white (or beluga) whales, and sperm whales roamed the sea. Since then, millions have been destroyed and all of these species are endangered. Laws have been passed to protect whales, but *whalers* (whale hunters) still kill thousands every year.

The prairie dog is a nuisance to farmers and ranchers because it eats crops and the grasses that cattle feed on. Millions of prairie dogs have been killed, and their numbers have been sharply reduced.

A great many animals have been killed, not for their fur or meat, or because they bother anyone, but just because some people enjoy killing

◀ Gorillas are threatened by the cutting down of the African forests.

▲ **Birds such as the egret were once hunted for their feathers.**

them. In the 1500s, Portuguese sailors clubbed to death the thousands of clumsy flightless dodo birds living on the island of Mauritius. More recently, the whooping crane and the sea otter have been almost completely killed off by hunters.

Mountain gorillas are the biggest and strongest of human relatives. But they are also rather quiet and lazy *vegetarians* (plant eaters) and will not bother any animal that does not bother them. In the push to develop Africa, people have destroyed many of the areas where gorillas live and have driven them into more crowded or less suitable places. The mountain gorilla is in danger of dying out because it cannot adapt to these new living places.

Peregrine falcons are fast flyers and clever hunters. They would appear to be natural survivors. But their numbers have decreased, which happened in a very strange way. Many farmers sprayed their crops with DDT, a powerful insecticide. Small animals ate the crops and swallowed the DDT. The peregrine falcons ate the animals and got the DDT into their own systems. The DDT weakened the shells of the eggs the falcons laid. The eggshells cracked before the young falcons were ready to hatch, and they died. Peregrine falcons thus became rare. DDT is now banned in the U.S.

If we don't want rare animals to become extinct animals, we must protect them. Laws must be passed to stop the intentional killing of endangered animals. The animals' natural homes must be *preserved* (saved), and protected areas must be set aside for animals whose natural homesites have been destroyed. Many programs are in existence to do this in the U.S.

◁ **In some parts of the world, snakes and alligators are still being killed for their skins, which are used to make shoes and handbags, but more and more countries now forbid this trade.**

There are also national and international agencies, such as the World Wildlife Fund and Greenpeace, that focus attention on the plight of endangered species. They lobby governments to pass conservation legislation and encourage international cooperation in controlling activities such as whaling and seal slaughter. Many countries have passed laws controlling the commercial import and export of animals.

Animals can take care of themselves if they are left alone. On a few small islands off New Zealand live lizardlike reptiles called tuataras. They are gentle, lazy animals that take 20 years to become adults. They would be prime candidates for extinction if they had any enemies or if more ambitious animals lived nearby. But about their only neighbors on the island are petrels—seabirds—and the petrels share their nests with the tuataras. Living in

> The rarest mammal is probably the Tasmanian wolf or thylacine. This marsupial has a head like a dog and hind quarters rather like a kangaroo. The animals were once numerous in Australia, but have been almost completely wiped out. However, a few sightings have been reported in Tasmania.

▲ **Although the fur trade is in decline, spotted cats like the South American margay are still killed for their fur, which is made into coats.**

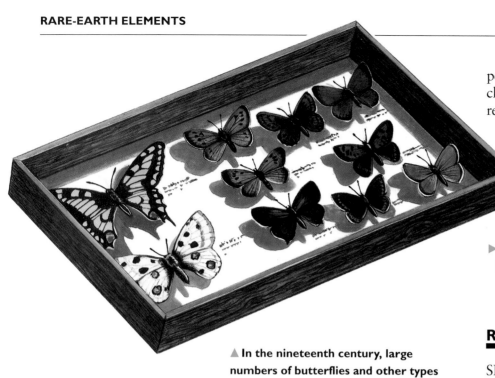

▲ In the nineteenth century, large numbers of butterflies and other types of insects were taken by collectors for displays like the one pictured here.

peace and quiet, the tuatara has not changed in 200 million years. Only recently, when people began hunting it for its meat and hide, was the tuatara in danger. But now it is protected by law. The tuatara is ecologically restricted, and it is rare, but fortunately it is not endangered.

▶▶▶▶ **FIND OUT MORE** ◀◀◀◀
Birds of the Past; Ecology; Mammals of the Past; Whales and Whaling

RARE-EARTH ELEMENTS

SEE ELEMENT

RATS AND MICE

Rats and mice that originally came from the Old World belong to the family of rodents called Muridae. Rats and mice native to the Americas are in a different rodent family, Cricetidae. All these rodents are alike in certain ways. Rats are usually bigger than mice, but both animals are furry, with long hairless tails and pointed ears and snouts. Both can be destructive pests.

Rats

There were no rats in North and South America before the Europeans arrived. Rats from the colonists' ships came ashore and began to breed. Rats multiply rapidly. Female rats begin breeding when only five months old. They give birth to litters of from 8 to 14 ratlings about five times a year. Rats are usually nocturnal, hunting for food at night and sleeping by day.

Rats have many habits and other characteristics in common with human beings. Rats can eat a great variety of food, as do people. Rats can live in many different environments—forests, deserts, mountains, and cities—as people do. Rats are

SOME RARE AND DEPLETED SPECIES

Animal	Distribution
Columbian white-tailed deer	Northwestern United States
Gray wolf	North America
Red kangaroo	Australia
Polar bear	Arctic regions
Giant panda	Tibet
Atlantic walrus	Northwestern Atlantic and Arctic Ocean
Black rhinoceros	Africa
White rhinoceros	Africa
Asiatic buffalo	Warmer countries of Asia
California gray whale	North Pacific
Bald eagle	North America
Peregrine falcon	Found in many parts of the world
Fin whale	Found in many oceans
West Indian manatee	West Indies and Central America
Leopard	Southern Asia and Africa
Ross seal	Antarctica
Pygmy hippopotamus	Liberia in Africa
California condor	Western United States
Mexican duck	Rio Grande Valley in Mexico
Galápagos flightless cormorant	Galápagos Islands
Whooping crane	North America
Desert tortoise	Western United States
Nilotic crocodile	Africa
Green turtle	Found in warm seas
Loggerhead turtle	Found in warm parts of the Atlantic Ocean
Tiger	Southern Asia

subject to many of the same diseases that people contract. Rats are aggressive and will fight and kill their own kind, just as human beings do. Most other mammals will not kill their own kind.

The two most common types of rat are the *brown rat* (sometimes called the *Norway rat)* and the *black rat.* The brown rat is larger and bolder than the black rat. It has grayish brown fur and measures about 16 inches (40 cm) in length, including its 7½-inch-long (19-cm-long) tail. The brown rat lives underground—in burrows, sewers, cellars, subways, and under houses and barns. The brown rat is a pest, attacking crops, domestic animals, and sometimes people.

The black rat is only about half as large as the brown rat and is less aggressive. The black rat was brought to the United States aboard ships in about the 1500s. The brown rat was brought in later and has driven the black rat out of many areas. Most black rats now live in tropical and subtropical climates.

Both the black and brown rat are harmful to human beings. They eat and spoil food in warehouses and on farms. They carry diseases, such as typhus fever and bubonic plague, that are dangerous to people. Because rats and people have so much in common, the *albino* (white strains) of both brown and black rats are bred for scientific study. By using rats, scientists are able to run tests on diet, medicines, diseases, growth, heredity, learning processes, and many other factors. Experimentation on rats helps scientists make discoveries that will aid people.

Other varieties of rats include the *roof rat,* a type of black rat that has migrated from Egypt to other warm areas of the world. The *bush* or *wood* rats are edible. They live far

from human habitation in forests and deserts. They eat only plants. The *pack rat* of the South Atlantic coast and the coast of the Gulf of Mexico collects objects—especially shiny ones—in its burrow. The *bushy-tailed wood rat* lives west of the Rocky Mountains and has a very furry tail.

▲ The common brown rat is a pest. It is a health hazard and can spread disease.

◀ The black rat is sometimes called the ship rat. It is often found at seaports and on board seagoing vessels.

Mice

Like rats, mice are found in great numbers throughout the world. They, too, can live in many different environments. Female mice breed every 10 to 17 weeks all year round, and they can have from five to ten young in each litter. Mice are harmful to people in much the same way as rats are. Albino mice are also used in scientific experiments.

There are hundreds of varieties of mice. Perhaps the best-known mouse is the common *house mouse.* This furry little creature lives in buildings, as well as in fields and forests. House mice that live outdoors are about 6½ inches (17 cm) long, including their tails. They eat insects and the roots,

▲ Deer mice, also called white-footed mice, are found all over North America, as is the house mouse (below).

◀ The meadow jumping mouse can leap a distance of 5 feet (1.5 m) or more. It uses a burrow only when it hibernates.

RONALD WILSON REAGAN FORTIETH PRESIDENT

JANUARY 20,1981– JANUARY 20,1989

Born: February 6, 1911, Tampico, Illinois

Parents: John Edward and Nellie Wilson Reagan

Education: Eureka College, Eureka, Illinois

Religion: Christian Church (Disciples of Christ)

Occupation: Actor and politician

State represented: California

Political party: Republican

Married: 1940 to Jane Wyman (born 1914); divorced, 1948. 1952 to Nancy Davis (born 1923)

Children: 1 daughter, 1 son (adopted) by first wife; 1 daughter, 1 son by second wife

leaves, and seeds of plants. Outdoor house mice usually come out only at night. House mice that live in buildings are slightly larger than those living outdoors because they usually have more food available to them. They like everything from ice cream and beer to soap and paste.

House mice are yellowish gray on top, often streaked with black, with a lighter gray underneath. Outdoor house mice build underground nests that they line with grass. Indoor house mice build nests in attics, basements, and inside walls, also lining them with soft materials.

Other varieties of mice include the *white-footed mouse*, which is slightly larger than the house mouse and has four white patches on its feet. The *cotton mouse* is found in the southern United States where it damages cotton crops by feeding on the plants and seedlings. The *grasshopper mouse* of the western states feeds almost entirely on insects and spiders. The *field mouse* is not really a mouse at all. It is a *vole*—a type of rodent that looks like a mouse but has a shorter tail. The *pocket mouse* is not a mouse either. It belongs to a genus of rodents that have fur-lined cheek pouches.

▶ ▶ ▶ ▶ **FIND OUT MORE** ◀ ◀ ◀ ◀
Animal; Animal Distribution; Animal Homes; Mammal; Pet; Rodent

READING

SEE LITERACY

REAGAN, RONALD WILSON (1911–   )

Ronald Reagan, a conservative Republican from California, won the U.S. Presidential election in 1980. His running mate, George Bush, was elected Vice President.

Reagan was born in Tampico, Illinois. After graduating from college,

▲ Ronald Reagan with Mikhail Gorbachev, last leader of the former Soviet Union. They worked together to reduce the number of nuclear arms.

he worked as a radio sportscaster for five years. At the time, he was a liberal Democrat, supporting President Franklin Roosevelt. From 1937 to 1966, Reagan worked as a movie and television actor. He headed the Screen Actors Guild and the Motion Picture Industry Council in the 1940s and 1950s. Reagan was a U.S. Army officer during World War II.

His politics gradually became conservative, and in 1962, Reagan formally declared himself a Republican. He was elected governor of California in 1966 and reelected in 1970. Many business leaders supported Reagan's policy for government spending cuts.

Upon becoming President, Reagan sought to fulfill his campaign promises. Financial aid to unsuccessful government programs was reduced, and tax cuts were passed by Congress. Reagan sought to balance the budget, but he let the deficit increase greatly. He strengthened the U.S. military defense, which was a major cause of the increased deficit. He fired striking air-traffic controllers

and appointed the first woman to the U.S. Supreme Court. An attempt to assassinate Reagan failed in 1981, and he was reelected by an overwhelming majority in 1984.

In 1987, Reagan signed an historic treaty with Soviet leader Mikhail Gorbachev. The pact aimed to reduce the storehouse of nuclear arms. In 1989, Reagan was succeeded by his Vice President, George Bush. Reagan was one of the most popular U.S. Presidents of all time. He still makes many public appearances.

▶ ▶ ▶ ▶ **FIND OUT MORE** ◀ ◀ ◀ ◀
Bush, George Herbert Walker;
Carter, James Earl, Jr.

REALISM

Many artists in the mid-1800s were painting pictures of imaginary people and places. This trend, called Romanticism, did not suit a French artist named Gustave Courbet. Courbet felt that artists should paint not imaginary scenes but real scenes of real life. Courbet began to paint in what is called a realistic manner. In 1849, he painted *The Stone Breakers*. This painting (destroyed in World War II) showed the backs of two men hard at work breaking stone. It was a truthful scene—not a romantic fantasy.

Courbet had a one-man show of his paintings in a shack in Paris in 1855. He called the exhibition "Realism, G. Courbet." Truth was what he was looking for in painting. He felt that truth lay in Realism—painting life the way it really was.

Shown on this page is a landscape by Courbet, *Beach in Normandy*. This scene is not *idealized* (made to seem perfect and beautiful) as the Romantics would have shown it. The tide is out, and the boats sit beached until high tide comes to float them. A Romantic painter would have put in a beautiful sunset, brought in the tide, or perhaps even changed the boats into large ships or barks of a mythological character.

Another painter who turned to painting everyday life was Jean François Millet. He liked painting figures. He wanted to show the poor peasants in the fields as they really looked. His idea was rather shocking because at this time most artists painted rich people gracefully posed. Look at his painting shown here, *The Sower*. The sower moves deliberately with a steady rhythm sowing the field, while the birds fly behind, looking for any seed they might pick up. Millet does not make the sower look elegant, but like a solid, hard-working French peasant. You can see that Millet respected sowing as an important action. But he does not try to make it romantic or pretty. He makes it seem true to life. Millet made painters aware of the beauty of common people doing everyday tasks. In a way, Realism paved the way for Impressionism, the movement in which artists became even more aware of everyday scenes and the light and weather at various times of day.

▶ ▶ ▶ ▶ **FIND OUT MORE** ◀ ◀ ◀ ◀
Impressionism; Romantic Period

▲ *Beach in Normandy*, **by Gustave Courbet, National Gallery of Art, Washington, D. C., Chester Dale Collection.**

▲ *The Sower*, **by the French painter Jean François Millet.**

RECIPE

SEE COOKING

RECONSTRUCTION

The effort made by Congress between 1865 and 1877 to rebuild the war-torn South just after the Civil War is called the period of Reconstruction. The defeated South had many problems. Cities and farms had been destroyed or badly damaged. There was little food or money. State and local governments were in a confused condition.

The Civil War had freed the black people. They were no longer slaves who could be owned and treated like a piece of property. Freedmen (as ex-slaves were then called) needed land, money, and education to get started in their new roles as free citizens. But former slaves had none of these things. They could not even serve on juries, testify in court, or vote—the basic rights of any U.S. citizen. If black people were to survive as freedmen, help had to come from the North. The black people's first problem was to get white Southerners to accept them as free people.

The Legacy of War
During the Civil War, 11 Southern states had split off from the United States. They had formed a separate nation, calling themselves the Confederate States of America. After the war, some Northern members of Congress felt that Southerners should be punished for having left the Union. President Lincoln and his suc-

cessor, President Andrew Johnson, felt that the Confederate States should be welcomed back into the Union with as little bitterness as possible. They decided that the Confederate States should be helped in *reconstructing* (rebuilding) their lands and local governments. These Presidents also declared that all freedmen must be ensured their rights as individuals.

The Proclamation of Amnesty and Reconstruction was issued by President Lincoln in 1863, in the midst of the war. He offered pardon to Confederate people who would promise to support the Constitution. The Confederate States could reenter the Union as soon as one-tenth of their voters had made this promise and set up a state government. After the war, Northern members of Congress set even stricter terms for the reentry of Southern states into the Union. Every Confederate state had to *ratify* (approve) the newly written Thirteenth, Fourteenth, and Fifteenth amendments to the Constitution. The Thirteenth Amendment declared slavery illegal in the United States. The Fourteenth Amendment gave blacks full rights as free citizens. The Fifteenth Amendment gave all male citizens the right to vote.

Southern legislators refused to ratify the new amendments. White political leaders especially disliked the Fourteenth and Fifteenth amendments. All kinds of ways were devised to keep freedmen from voting, holding office, or otherwise using their citizenship rights. Southern whites voted each other into office.

When the thirty-ninth Congress met in Washington, D.C., in December 1865, representatives and senators from the South included the vice president of the former Confederate States, 4 Confederate generals, 5 Confederate colonels, 6 members of the Confederate cabinet, and 58 members of the Confederate States Congress. None of these persons had

▼ During the period of Reconstruction, many black people were elected to political office in the South. Hiram R. Revels (left) from Mississippi was the first black U.S. Senator. Here he is shown with U.S. representatives (second from left to right) Benjamin Turner of Alabama, Robert DeLarge of South Carolina, Josiah Walls of Florida, Jefferson Long of Georgia, and Joseph Rainy and Robert Brown Elliot of South Carolina.

approved the Constitutional amendments, and none was in sympathy with citizenship for black people. These former Confederates were not allowed seats in Congress and so returned home to take charge at state and local levels. There they passed laws that blocked the rights of former slaves. Blacks could not testify in court and could not travel without a permit. Blacks who had no jobs were arrested and made to pay a large fine. If unable to pay, blacks were handed over to employers who paid the fine and then forced blacks to work for them. In this way, thousands of blacks were forced into a new kind of slavery.

The Freedmen's Bureau

On March 3, 1865, the Freedmen's Bureau was established. The bureau's job included the feeding and clothing of war refugees. The bureau set up schools for blacks and supplied medical services for all in need. It managed lands and other property that were deserted by or taken from Confederates during the Civil War. One of the bureau's most important jobs was the supervision of contracts between freedmen and their white employers (who were often the blacks' former masters).

To make sure Southern states accepted the new Constitutional amendments, Congress passed the Reconstruction Act of 1867. This law divided the former Confederate States into five military districts, each governed by a Northern army commander. Thousands of black voters, supported and defended by U.S. troops, went to the polls and began voting former Confederates out of state and local offices. New officials took their places. Some were dishonest white Northerners, called *carpetbaggers,* who came to the South to make money out of the mixed-up conditions. Some were white Southerners, called *scalawags,* who sided with the North. But many of these

new officials were black people. They ranged from highly educated to poor and *illiterate* (unable to read or write). Some were cautious officials, and some were bold and daring. Some felt sorry for the defeated Confederates, and others were angry and bitter. These new black leaders were elected to state and local governments and to the U.S. Congress.

From 1867 to 1877, Reconstruction legislatures made great changes in the laws. They wrote new state constitutions, ensuring civil rights for all, that lasted for many years. They did away with laws that sent people to jail because they owed money. They established free public schools for everyone, and they ratified the three new amendments to the Constitution. But the accomplishments of these legislatures were drowned out by white Confederates who accused black leaders of *corruption* (illegal dealings). These charges had a terrible effect, because people began to believe them. Some black officials *were* corrupt—but so were many whites. The North was getting tired of spending money and sympathy on the "Southern problem" that never seemed to end. White Southerners, who had been used to low taxes before the war, were furious at being taxed by black legislators to provide money for schools and new roads.

▲ This Freedmen's Bureau primary school in Vicksburg, Mississippi, was set up to provide former slaves with an education, so that they could qualify for better jobs and could exercise their full rights as U.S. citizens.

◀ This cartoon depicts a "carpetbagger." The term was used to describe Northern adventurers seeking fortune and political power in the defeated Southern states, in the period called Reconstruction, after the Civil War. They carried their possessions in carpetbags. Many carpetbaggers were, in fact, honest people who went south to help build up the South's crippled economy, educational system, and government.

One of the most frightening organizations to spring up during the Reconstruction period was the Ku Klux Klan. It began in Pulaski, Tennessee, in 1866 and soon spread throughout the South. Members of the Klan draped themselves and their horses in white sheets and rode around at night killing and terrifying blacks and people who sympathized with them. Factions of the Klan still exist today.

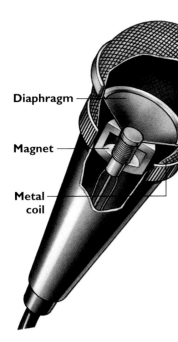

▲ In a microphone, sound is changed into electric signals. Sound waves set the diaphragm vibrating, creating an electric current in the metal coil.

Diaphragm

Magnet

Metal coil

2228

White Power Restored

By 1869, former Confederate officials, white landowners, and out-of-work politicians were determined to regain control of their states, even if it meant working with poor whites, called *rednecks*. The idea was to use any way possible—from speeches to murder—to restore white power. Black citizens began to be attacked by terrorist gangs of night riders, such as the Ku Klux Klan, the Knights of the White Camellia, and the Red Shirts. They whipped and murdered blacks and any whites who supported civil rights for blacks.

Soon, black people were defeated in elections or forced out of office by white terrorist groups. White Confederates took control of North Carolina in 1870, Texas in 1873, Arkansas and Alabama in 1874, Mississippi in 1875, South Carolina in 1876, and Florida and Louisiana in 1877. They had already expelled blacks from the Georgia legislature (1868) and taken control of Tennessee in 1869.

The Presidential election of 1876 killed once and for all the hopes of equality for Southern blacks. Samuel Tilden (the Democratic candidate favored by Southern whites) ran against Republican Rutherford B. Hayes. When votes were counted, a dispute arose over the number of votes cast in Oregon, Louisiana, Florida, and South Carolina. Republican leaders and Southern officials agreed to give the election to Hayes. But it is thought that Southern leaders agreed to accept Hayes if he would, as President, give the South financial aid. In order to get Hayes elected, Republicans also agreed to withdraw the last federal troops from the South.

As the troops disappeared, so did any further attempts at Reconstruction. The hopes of freed black people for civil rights, schools, paying jobs, and real dignity were silenced for almost 100 years.

▶ ▶ ▶ ▶ **FIND OUT MORE** ◀ ◀ ◀ ◀
American History; Black Americans; Civil Rights; Civil Rights Movement; Civil War; Confederate States of America; Constitution, United States; Hayes, Rutherford B.; Johnson, Andrew; Lincoln, Abraham

☼ RECORDING

If you love music, you can listen to your favorite tunes or songs wherever you are. You can have a disc or cassette player at home and in the car, or you can carry your own personal player with you. This wealth of music is made possible by sound recording. In addition, most of the music you hear on the radio and television is music that has been recorded. A video is a recording of vision, as in television pictures, as well as of sound.

Thomas Alva Edison invented sound recording in 1877. He built the first phonograph, which played wax cylinders with grooves like those on an LP or single record. The record player is a direct descendant of Edison's phonograph. However, like other kinds of players, it produces sound in a different way.

How Sound Recording Works

There are several different systems for recording sound, but they all work in the same general way. First, a microphone changes the sound waves in speech, song, or music into electric signals. These audio or sound signals are then stored on a tape or disc. When the tape or disc is played, the player produces the electric signals again. They go to an amplifier, which makes the signals stronger so that they can travel along wires and power a speaker or earphones.

In recording, the sound signals are stored in four different ways. On LP or single records, the signals are stored as the wiggles in the groove on the surface of the record. On a com-

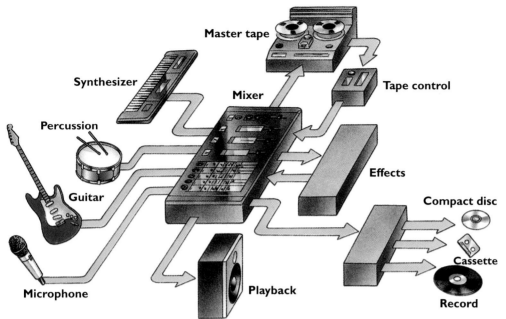

Master tape

Synthesizer

Percussion

Mixer

Tape control

Guitar

Effects

Compact disc

Microphone

Playback

Cassette

Record

◀ **In a recording studio, the sounds of voices and instruments can be mixed electronically, and then remixed, adding special effects if necessary. This continues until the engineers are satisfied with the sound produced on the master tape. The master tape is then used to make vinyl records, cassette tapes, or compact discs.**

pact disc, the signals are in the form of patterns of tiny holes in the surface. On tape cassettes and reels of tape, the sound signals are stored as magnetic patterns in a magnetic coating on the tape. The sound in a motion picture is recorded as light and dark patterns in a track at the side of the film.

A complete stereo system has almost all the equipment you need to play any recording that you can buy. It has a record player to play LP and single records, one or two tape players to play back tape cassettes and to record sounds on tape, a compact disc player, a radio, an amplifier, and two loudspeakers, plus a headphone connection. It may also have a graphic equalizer, which allows you to alter the tone of the sounds.

Tape Recording

In a recording studio, singers and musicians record their music on a large tape recorder. This is like a cassette player, but uses big reels of tape. Each microphone sends an electric signal to the tape recorder. The record head in the tape recorder contains an electromagnet that converts the electric signal into a magnetic field that varies in strength. The magnetic tape moves past the record head. In the surface of the tape are

millions of tiny metal particles. The magnetic field magnetizes the particles so that the electric sound signal is stored on the tape as a magnetic pattern. The tape recorder also has a replay head, which converts the magnetic pattern back into an electric sound signal as the tape moves past it.

A big tape recorder used in a recording studio has as many as 24 record heads and 24 replay heads. It can record the sound signals from 24 microphones or electronic instruments, such as synthesizers, in 24 separate tracks on the tape. The tape is then used to make a master tape. All the signals from the big recorder are mixed together to make a master tape. This has only two tracks—one each for the two loudspeakers in a stereo player. Records, compact

▼ **1. Most cassettes contain plastic tape coated with iron oxide. The iron oxide particles are in a random pattern, but when the tape passes through the record head, the particles are magnetized and formed into a magnetic pattern to store sounds. The replay head turns the magnetic pattern back into electrical signals. These signals are then amplified to produce sounds. 2. The erase head erases a previous magnetic pattern (recording). The record head creates a new pattern.**

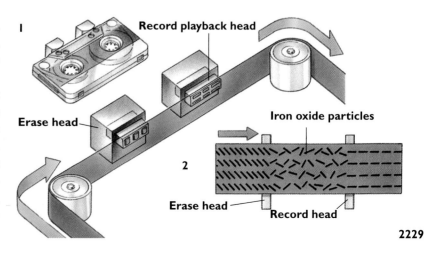

1

Record playback head

Erase head

Iron oxide particles

2

Erase head

Record head

▼ A typical home stereo system consists of inputs, an amplifier and a control unit, and outputs (top right diagram). The inputs detect coded signals in a variety of forms, turn them into electrical signals, and feed them to the amplifier. In stereo records, the signals are coded as bumps and waves in a V-shaped groove. These signals are picked up by the stylus.

MAGNETIC PICK-UP FOR VINYL DISC

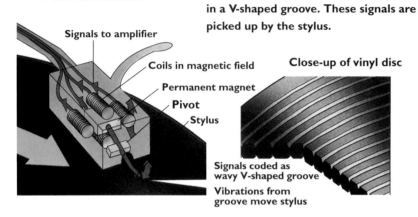

Signals to amplifier

Coils in magnetic field

Permanent magnet

Pivot

Stylus

Close-up of vinyl disc

Signals coded as wavy V-shaped groove

Vibrations from groove move stylus

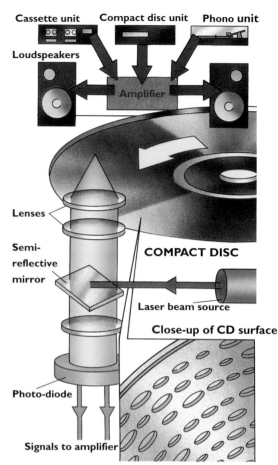

Cassette unit   Compact disc unit   Phono unit

Loudspeakers

Amplifier

Lenses

Semi-reflective mirror

COMPACT DISC

Laser beam source

Close-up of CD surface

Photo-diode

Signals to amplifier

▲ A compact disc track contains a pattern of tiny pits which store sounds in coded form. As the disc spins in the player, it is scanned by a laser, and the beam is turned into electrical pulses.

Crystals such as quartz behave in an interesting way. If an alternating electric current is passed through them, they vibrate in time with the changing flow of the current. This effect is used to make very accurate clocks and to keep broadcasting transmitters at exactly the right frequency. The effect works the other way, too. If these crystals (called piezoelectric) are made to vibrate very quickly, they produce an electric current of that frequency. It is crystals such as these that are used in phonograph pickups, to change the vibrations of the needle in the record groove into electric current for the amplifier.

discs, and cassette tapes are then made from this master tape, or the master tape may be broadcast over the radio.

A tape player uses tape cassettes. These have four tracks—two going one way and two going the other—so that the cassette has stereo music on both sides. There is usually just one head that records or replays. An erase head wipes out an old recording before a new one is made. It produces a magnetic field that removes any magnetic pattern from the tape.

Records

When a record is made, the electric signals from the master tape go to a machine that cuts a wiggly groove into a master disc. The disc spins at 33⅓ or 45 rpm (revolutions per minute). The records that people buy are copies of this disc.

When a record is played, a *stylus*, or needle, is placed in the groove. As the record spins, the stylus vibrates. A *pickup* (cartridge) attached to the stylus produces the electric signals that then go to an amplifier. Records are rapidly being replaced by audio cassettes and most recently by compact discs.

Compact discs

When a compact disc (CD) is made, the electric signals from the master tape are transferred to a machine containing a laser. They cause the laser beam to flash on and off extremely quickly, and the laser burns a spiral track of millions of tiny holes in a spinning aluminum disc.

To play back sound from a compact disc, the disc is placed in a CD player, where it is spun at about 4 revolutions per second. A beam of laser light follows the spiral track of tiny holes, and relays the change in the amount of light reflected to a photodetector. This changes the light to a series of on-off electrical pulses, which are the same as those on the master tape.

Analog and Digital

There are two basic kinds of ways in which sound is recorded: analog and digital. Records are recorded by the analog method, compact discs use digital sound recording, and tapes can be recorded using either analog or digital. Digital recording results in a higher quality of sound.

In digital recording, a computer measures the changing voltage of the electric sound signal from the microphone thousands of times a second. It converts the measurements into code numbers. In the player, a computer changes the code numbers back into an electric sound signal.

In analog recording, the recording—a wiggly groove or magnetic pattern—is a direct copy of the electric sound signal in another form. As the voltage changes, the groove or pattern changes, too.

▶▶▶▶ **FIND OUT MORE** ◀◀◀◀
Compact Disc; Edison, Thomas Alva; Electronics; Music; Sound; Video

RECYCLING

Do you throw things away into special trash bags or barrels? Perhaps these different kinds of refuse are collected on special days in your neighborhood. Maybe you take bottles, paper, and aluminum cans to collection points in your community. All of these measures are part of a plan to recycle waste materials.

▶ **Our society throws away a lot of unwanted items that could be reclaimed and reused. Many valuable materials, which could be saved and recycled, go to your local dump.**

Recycling is a way of processing wastes to remove matter that can be reused. Recycled ingredients can be used to manufacture similar products. That has two main advantages. One is that people think twice about throwing things away and creating litter.

The second advantage is that it helps the environment by using recycled material to manufacture new products. For years, scientists have warned that the world will use up all of its raw ingredients unless new methods are devised to limit their use.

Some industries, such as paper, iron, and steel, have been recycling goods for nearly 100 years.

The wider public has become involved in recycling since the 1960s. Federal, state, and local governments have responded to this public concern. For example, people in many states pay a deposit on each can or bottle they buy. When they return the empty can or bottle to a recycling center, they are refunded the deposit. Local recycling centers take paper, plastics, aluminum, textiles, and glass. Many dumps and landfills separate trash into

■ Paper and cardboard
■ Vegetable matter
■ Plastics
□ Textiles
■ Glass
■ Dust and cinders
■ Other
■ Metals

▲ **Above are the proportions of different materials in domestic rubbish. A large part of domestic rubbish is paper and cardboard, which could easily be recycled.**

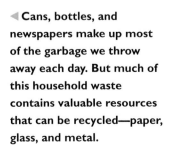

◀ **Cans, bottles, and newspapers make up most of the garbage we throw away each day. But much of this household waste contains valuable resources that can be recycled—paper, glass, and metal.**

similar categories.

New methods are constantly being developed to recycle more goods or to recycle goods more efficiently. Glass can be ground up and reused. Paper can also be recycled or turned into other industrial ingredients. Motor oil can be recycled as heavy-duty industrial oil. Even some sorts of garbage can be reused as fertilizer!

▶ ▶ ▶ ▶ **FIND OUT MORE** ◀ ◀ ◀ ◀
Ecology; Iron and Steel;
Waste Disposal

Red Cross

Red Crescent

Magen David

▲ **The Red Cross has different names and symbols in different parts of the world. In some Muslim countries, it is the Red Crescent. In Israel, the symbol is the Magen David.**

 ## RED CROSS

A patient who needs blood in a New York hospital and a victim of an earthquake in Iran may each be helped by the Red Cross. Caring *about* and caring *for* others are ideals shared by the International Committee of the Red Cross, the League of Red Cross Societies, and more than 120 national Red Cross, Red Crescent, Red Magen David, and Red Lion and Sun societies—all of whom belong to the Red Cross.

In 1859, a Swiss banker named Jean Henri Dunant was on a trip in Italy. He was very troubled by the suffering he saw on the battlefield during the Austro-Sardinian War. Dunant originated the idea of forming voluntary national societies for the care of ill and wounded soldiers during war—no matter on whose side they were fighting. One result of Dunant's efforts was the Geneva Convention of 1864. This treaty between nations began the Red Cross movement. Today, prisoners of war, the wounded and sick, and civilians are all under the protection of the Geneva Convention.

In 1881, Clara Barton began the organization now known as the American Red Cross (ARC).

▶ ▶ ▶ ▶ **FIND OUT MORE** ◀ ◀ ◀ ◀
Barton, Clara

 ## RED SEA

The Red Sea is a body of water that is almost closed in by land. It separates the Arabian peninsula and northeastern Africa.

The Red Sea lies between the sandy shores of Saudi Arabia on the east and Egypt, Sudan, and Ethiopia on the west. At its southern end, the Red Sea reaches the Gulf of Aden and the Arabian Sea through a narrow channel. (See the map with the article on the MIDDLE EAST.)

At its northern end, the Red Sea branches in two directions, separated by the Sinai Peninsula. The Gulf of Aqaba leads to the Israeli port of Elath. The Gulf of Suez leads to the Suez Canal. When the canal opened in 1869, ships could then sail from Asia to Europe through the Mediterranean, making the extremely long voyage around Africa unnecessary.

The Red Sea is about 1,400 miles (2,250 km) long and up to 220 miles (355 km) wide. Its waters fill part of a large crack in the Earth's surface called the Great Rift. The Red Sea is more than 7,000 feet (2,135 m) deep in spots. Ship captains must navigate carefully to avoid large, dangerous coral reefs.

The sea may have received its name from the reddish algae that cover the water's surface in some

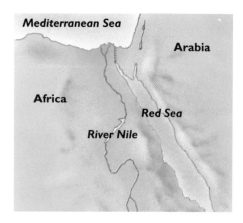

▲ **The Red Sea separates the continents of Africa and Asia. It is growing wider all the time. Scientists believe that one day it will become a giant ocean.**

▲ Looking toward the shores of Jordan in the Arabic peninsula, from the Gulf of Aqaba in the Red Sea.

places, making the water look red.

The Bible tells of Moses leading the Israelites through the Red Sea. Scholars believe that the Bible writer meant the "Sea of Reeds," a marshy area at the tip of the Gulf of Suez. Moses could have guided his followers on foot through this sea of reeds, but the pursuing Egyptian chariots would have bogged down in the marshy swamp.

▶ ▶ ▶ ▶ **FIND OUT MORE** ◀ ◀ ◀ ◀
Suez Canal

⚙ RED SHIFT

The tone of a police siren sounds lower as the police car moves away from you. The tone changes because the distance between the sound waves (the wavelength) increases. This is called the Doppler effect.

The Doppler effect also applies to light which also travels in waves. Light is detected across a spectrum, ranging from red (long waves) to violet (short waves). As objects move away, the distance between their light waves becomes greater. If the object moves away fast enough, the wavelength moves to the red part of the spectrum. This is called red shift.

Red shift can only be detected in objects traveling at very high speeds,

such as stars or galaxies. Only then does the object's speed begin to approach the speed of light itself.

Astronomers began noticing the red shifts of objects during the 1920s. In 1929, an American astronomer, Edwin Hubble, noted that the most distant objects in the universe had the greatest red shifts. Hubble's studies showed that these objects were moving away from us the fastest. This evidence lies at the heart of the Big Bang Theory, which argues that the universe began with a huge explosion, and everything is still moving out from the original blast.

▶ ▶ ▶ ▶ **FIND OUT MORE** ◀ ◀ ◀ ◀
Astronomy; Light;
Radio Astronomy; Spectrum

▼ Light from distant galaxies shows a shift toward the red end of the spectrum, because the galaxies are moving away at very high speeds and the distance between the light waves has increased.

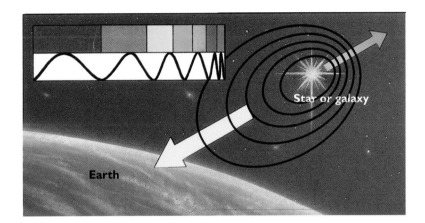

Star or galaxy

Earth

⚙ REED, WALTER (1851–1902)

Walter Reed was an American doctor who discovered the cause of yellow fever, and demonstrated how it could be controlled.

Walter Reed was born in Gloucester County, Virginia. He joined the United States Army Medical Corps in 1875. In 1893, he was made a professor at the Army Medical College in Washington, D.C.

The Spanish-American War broke out in 1898. Many American soldiers, who had been sent to Cuba to fight in the war, were dying of typhoid fever and yellow fever. Reed thought that flies and

▲ Walter Reed, U.S. Army Medical Corps doctor who discovered the cause of yellow fever.

▲ This student is learning to use a reference library, an important skill that will be useful in his studies now and in the future.

▼ A gathering of intellectuals in Paris in the 1750s that included Diderot, the French writer and philosopher, who compiled the first great encyclopedia. It was called simply the *Encyclopédie*, and it took Diderot 20 years to produce it.

dust caused the spread of typhoid fever. He recommended the camps be cleaned up.

When this proved successful, Reed was put in charge of a group of doctors who were in Cuba trying to find ways to control yellow fever, which was threatening the construction of the Panama Canal. Reed thought that the disease was carried by the bite of a mosquito. He carried out tests on soldier volunteers, who allowed themselves to be bitten by mosquitoes infected with yellow fever, and proved that he was correct. As a result of Reed's work, mosquitoes have been controlled and yellow fever has been nearly wiped out.

▶ ▶ ▶ ▶ **FIND OUT MORE** ◀ ◀ ◀ ◀
Disease; Medicine; Mosquito;
Spanish-American War

REED INSTRUMENTS

SEE WOODWIND INSTRUMENTS

REFERENCE BOOK

Nearly every home has a dictionary and a cookbook. These are two of the most common kinds of reference

books. Reference books are collections of information arranged (often in alphabetical order) so that a reader can easily refer to them to find the specific information he or she is searching for.

General Reference Books
General reference books are filled with information on many subjects. *Dictionaries* contain lists of words with their pronunciations, meanings, and origins. A *thesaurus* gives a list of words, and with them, words that have the same, similar, and opposite meanings. A thesaurus is useful when you cannot think of the exact word you need. General reference *encyclopedias* contain articles summarizing information in almost every field of study. An *atlas* is a collection of maps of a city, a country, or the world.

A *bibliography* is a reference book about other books. It contains lists of books and articles that provide information on a particular subject. Yearbooks, or *almanacs*, are published annually and contain important world information from the previous year.

Specialized Reference Books
Some reference books provide information on more specialized subjects. Foreign-language dictionaries give pronunciations and translate words from one language to another. Many dictionaries are even more specialized and provide meanings only for words in a particular field, such as music or medicine. Some encyclopedias contain articles on only one subject, such as astronomy. *Handbooks* and *guides* usually provide instruction about a certain activity, such as fishing, or information about a specific subject or place. Information about local, state, and federal governments is often given in *manuals, registers*, and *directories*. Certain reference books consist of brief biographies of famous people. For example, *Who's Who in America* contains biographies of well-known living Americans.

The Reference Section

Libraries contain areas devoted to reference books. The reference section in a library is often in a separate room. The reader cannot check out these books, so they will always be available for everyone to use.

▶▶▶▶ **FIND OUT MORE** ◀◀◀◀
Almanac; Atlas; Bibliography; Dictionary; Encyclopedia; Index; Library; Library of Congress

REFLECTION

SEE LIGHT, MIRROR

REFORMATION

SEE GERMAN HISTORY, PROTESTANT REFORMATION

REFRIGERATION

If you put some ice in an insulated chest full of warm food, the ice will slowly melt and the food will get colder. This happens because heat always moves from a warm body to a cold body. The heat in the warm food passes into the ice. This makes the ice warmer and causes it to melt. It makes the food colder because it now has less heat. This *transfer* (movement) of heat goes on until the ice has melted.

A refrigerator is more complicated than an ice chest, but it works in the same way. In a refrigerator a liquid, called a *refrigerant*, does the work of the ice, absorbing heat from inside the refrigerator. The liquid refrigerant is evaporated in *coils* (metal tubes). As it evaporates, the refrigerant picks up the heat from inside the refrigerator. Then the refrigerant is put under high pressure so that it changes back to a liquid and gives off the heat to the outside air. The same refrigerant is reused.

A refrigerator has thick insulated walls. Insulation prevents heat or cold from passing through a wall. A well insulated refrigerator does not run all the time. It has a *thermostat,* a combination thermometer and switch, that turns on the refrigerator when it gets too warm.

Foods, such as milk and meat, are refrigerated to keep them from spoiling. Many of the bacteria that spoil food cannot grow at temperatures below 40° or 50°F (4.4° or 10°C). The *maximum* (highest) safe temperature for storing foods that can spoil is 50°F (10°C). Food preserved by freezing will stay fresh longer. The temperature of a home freezer is usually about 0°F (-18°C).

▶▶▶▶ **FIND OUT MORE** ◀◀◀◀
Bacteria; Food; Food Processing; Gas; Heat and Cold; Liquid

REFUGEE

A *refugee* is a person who leaves his or her homeland to seek *refuge,* or shelter, in another country. A refugee often leaves a country to escape war or persecution. The term "refugee" also applies to people who have been left homeless because of war or natural disasters, such as earthquakes, famine, or floods. Refugees are considered refugees until they are reestablished in their own country or are living permanently and earning a living in a new country.

Refugees and *emigrants* are similar, but there is one important difference. Emigrants leave their homeland of their own free will. Refugees are forced to leave.

It was not difficult for a refugee to find a new place to live until the 1900s. Since then, finding homes for refugees has become an international problem. The United Nations has set up a commission to help find homes for refugees from wars and revolutions. Refugees who can find no

▲ **A refrigerator of the 1920s. Refrigerators first came into use in the 1860s.**

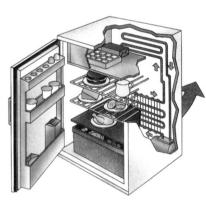

▲ **A refrigerator works by absorbing the heat from the inside and sending it to the outside. In an electric refrigerator, a special liquid is pumped through pipes to carry the heat out. First an evaporator inside the refrigerator absorbs the heat, then the heat is given out again by a condenser, which is a series of coils outside the refrigerator.**

▲ These two children are refugees from a famine in their country, Ethiopia. Civilians fleeing war or natural disaster are often made refugees in their own countries.

▼ Lizards shed their tails to get away from enemies like this hawk. The hawk is left with only a tail in its talons, while the lizard escapes. The lizard will soon grow a new, slightly shorter tail.

homes are often forced to live in refugee camps, where living conditions are difficult. More than a million Arab refugees from Palestine have lived in temporary camps in nearby lands since the Arab-Israeli War of 1948, when Palestine became Israel. Since 1980, many refugees have faced starvation in war-torn Lebanon. The U.S. government has recently helped many refugees from Vietnam, Cuba, and Haiti—especially those seeking political asylum.

▶▶▶▶ **FIND OUT MORE** ◀◀◀◀
Immigration; United Nations

REGENERATION

If your hair is cut, it soon grows back. Your fingernails continue to grow as long as you live. Hair and fingernails replace themselves, or *regenerate*. Among many kinds of animals, regeneration includes the ability to replace whole parts of the body. A lizard that loses its tail can grow a new one. A lobster can regenerate a missing claw.

Among higher animals, most examples of regeneration are everyday events. Human beings and other

mammals replace hair, skin, and claws. Birds grow new feathers at least once a year. Deer shed antlers and grow new ones. But human beings and other mammals cannot grow new limbs. Many lower animals, however, can do this.

Salamanders can sometimes replace lost legs or tails. If a salamander loses its entire leg, or a part of it, the wound quickly heals. Then a knob of tissue begins growing. Within a few weeks a complete leg has replaced the lost one. In certain lower animals, a whole new individ-

▲ Some animals can *regenerate* (regrow) new limbs or other parts of their bodies. This starfish can replace a lost arm, and its severed arm can even grow into a new starfish.

ual sometimes grows out of one piece of the old body. One arm of a starfish, if it has a piece of the center, can regenerate a whole new body. The hydra is a freshwater polyp that regenerates from a tiny section of its old body. Regeneration takes place in common earthworms. Earthworms are divided into sections, or segments, that can usually grow back if cut away.

Certain animals get rid of body parts deliberately in order to save themselves from enemies. Then they regenerate the lost part. If you pick up a lizard by its tail, the animal may escape by leaving its tail in your hand and scurrying off without it. Many lower animals, such as starfish, crabs, and some insects, avoid capture by letting their legs drop off.

▶▶▶▶ **FIND OUT MORE** ◀◀◀◀
Growth

RELATIVITY

Imagine that you are standing by the side of a road and a car passes by going 30 miles (50 km) per hour. You judge the speed by imagining that you are at rest and the car is moving. (In fact you know that you are not really at rest, because the Earth on which you stand is turning and moving around the sun. The sun itself is moving through space.) This is the basic idea of relativity: assuming that you are not moving and working out the speed of something that is moving *relative to* you.

You can easily think of other examples of relativity at work. For instance, if you are moving in a car at 30 miles (50 km) per hour and another car is approaching you at 40 miles (65 km) per hour, it seems to be coming toward you at 70 miles (115 km) per hour. We say that the second car is moving 70 miles per hour relative to the first car.

Toward the end of the last century, some very surprising results appeared in experiments on the speed of light. It seems that this speed is always the same no matter how fast the source of light moves. It is always 186,000 miles (300,000 km) per second.

In 1905, Albert Einstein introduced a theory of relative motion to explain this strange fact. The first part dealt with observations made about things moving in a straight line at a constant speed. It was called the *special* theory of relativity. One of the things Einstein assumed was that the speed of everything must be measured relative to the speed of light.

This may seem quite a simple idea in itself, but it had far-reaching effects on the ideas of science. Some implications were very strange. For instance, Einstein showed that the faster things move the more mass they have and the slower time seems to pass relative to time as measured by an outside observer. A person traveling in a fast-moving spaceship would age more slowly than a person on Earth. Another surprising result is that mass can be changed into energy. This is the source of power in the atom bomb.

Most of the implications of relativity are important only for things moving at very high speeds, close to the speed of light.

Later, in 1915, Einstein produced a second part of his theory, the *general* theory of relativity. This deals with objects that are slowing down or speeding up, or are moving in curved paths. This theory gives a better understanding of space, gravity, and the nature of the universe.

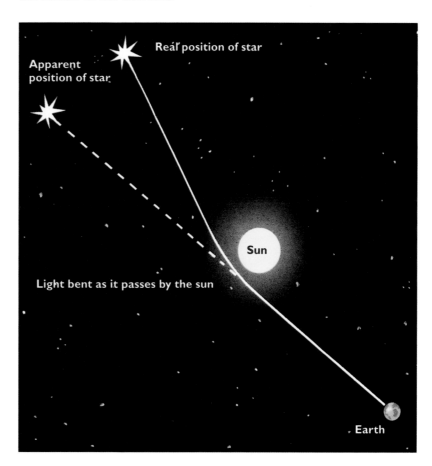

▲ Part of Einstein's theory of relativity says that matter in space exerts a force of gravity that distorts or "curves" the frame of reference in space. In other words, gravitational force is capable of bending a beam of light from a distant star. This means that when the light from the star is seen on earth, the star appears to be in a different position in the sky from its true position.

▶ ▶ ▶ ▶ **FIND OUT MORE** ◀ ◀ ◀ ◀
Einstein, Albert

▲ The crescent moon and star are the symbols of Islam's most holy book, the *Koran*. The Islamic religion was founded in Arabia by the prophet Muhammad.

▲ Hinduism is an ancient Indian religion with no known founder. Hindus worship many gods. The god symbolized above is Shiva, the destroyer, who rules over life and death.

▲ The Star of David, symbol of Judaism. Judaism was founded by Abraham and Moses and was the first religion to teach that there is one God.

RELIGION

Religion is people's belief in some power greater than themselves. This power is often called *God*. God or gods have been known by various names throughout history. In Hinduism, the greatest god is called *Brahman*. In Judaism, the god's name is *Yahweh or Jehovah*. The Muslims call their god *Allah*. Taoists believe in a supreme principle called *Tao*, meaning "The Way." Christians use the name *God*.

Basic Types of Religion

Throughout human history, three basic types of religion have developed. The earliest was *animism*, a belief that everything in nature has a spirit or soul of its own. Early people believed they were completely surrounded by these spirits—some of which were good, and some of which were evil. Human religion was aimed at encouraging the good spirits and protecting people from evil spirits. People held rain ceremonies, for example, so the rain spirit would water the crops. And they had ceremonies to make the evil spirits leave a sick person.

Polytheism is a belief in numerous gods. Each god ruled over certain areas of human life, such as war, love, agriculture, and health. The gods of polytheism were different from the spirits of animism. They were believed to have definite personalities, similar to those of human beings, and were not limited to living in natural objects. Tales were told about the deeds of these gods and goddesses. The mythologies of ancient Egypt, Greece, Rome, the Norse countries, the Aztecs, and the Navajos all contain legends about how the world was created or how mankind came to be. People believed they could influence the gods and make agreements with them to ensure pleasant or successful out-

comes in their lives. Hinduism is the greatest polytheistic religion in the world today.

Monotheism is the belief in one all-powerful god. Judaism, Christianity, and Islam are the three great monotheistic religions of the modern world. A god of monotheism is believed to be aware of everything that happens in the world. The monotheistic god is believed to have created the world. This god is also believed to be the judge of human behavior, determining whether a person has lived a good and holy life or not.

Most religions do not fit neatly into one or

◄ The symbol of Christianity is the cross. Christianity is based on the life and teachings of Jesus Christ.

another of these types. Hinduism, for example, is a polytheistic religion, but Hindus also believe in one supreme god, Brahman, who is greater than all of the others. The teachings of Buddha do not even mention a god, but Buddha stressed that people must treat each other with kindness in order to gain peace for themselves and for the world.

The various religions throughout the modern world are different not only in their gods but also in how believers worship them. Each religion usually has certain writings that are considered sacred: the Bible (Judaism—Old Testament; Christianity—Old and New Testament), the Koran (Islam), the Bhagavad-Gita (Hinduism), the Tripitaka (Buddhism), and the Tao Te Ching (Taoism). Each religion usually has one or more holy persons, or saints, who have inspired the faith of the people. In nearly every religion

◄ Buddhists make many statues of the Buddha.

MAJOR RELIGIONS IN THE WORLD TODAY

Name	Founder	Where Founded	When Founded	Where Found Today	Name of Followers
Buddhism	Gautama Buddha (about 563–483 B.C.)	India	About 500 B.C.	Cambodia, Laos, Vietnam, Thailand, Burma, China, Japan, Korea	Buddhists
Christianity	Jesus Christ (about 4 B.C.–A.D. 29)	Palestine (now Israel)	About A.D.. 29	Mostly in Europe, Africa, North & South America, Australia	Christians
Confucianism	Confucius (551–478 B.C.)	China	400s B.C.	China	Confucians
Hinduism	Founder unknown	India	Between 3000 and 1500 B.C.	Mainly in India	Hindus
Islam	Muhammad (A.D. 570–632)	Arabia	A.D. 600s	Middle East, North Africa, Western Asia	Muslims
Judaism	Abraham (about 1700s B.C.)	Canaan (now Israel)	1700s B.C.	Mainly in U.S., Europe, Israel	Jews
Shintoism	Founder unknown	Japan	500s B.C.	Japan	Shintoists
Taoism	Lao-tse (about 604–531 B.C.)	China	500s B.C.	China	Taoists

there are various *sects*, or branches. These are groups who believe in the basic faith of the religion but differ in how they follow or practice the religion. The Methodists, Presbyterians, Lutherans, Episcopalians, Greek Orthodox, and Catholics are some of the sects of Christianity. The Conservative, Reform, and Orthodox congregations are sects of Judaism.

Prayer and Sacrifice

In all religions, believers feel themselves to have a relationship with their god or gods. What people do or don't do makes a difference in what will happen between them and their god. For this reason, almost all religions have some form of prayer. Prayer is people's way of speaking to their god. People use prayer to ask their god for help or protection. They also use prayer to praise their god and to thank their god for what has

been done. In many religions, prayer is simply *meditation*—a way of getting to understand and know the god by silently thinking or contemplating about the god.

When people believe in a god, they sometimes feel they must give the god something. This is called *sacrifice*. People usually sacrifice to a god something that is very important to them. Early people used to sacrifice the first grains of their harvest or the first animals born in their flocks. This showed that they were willing to sacrifice something as important as their food in order to please the god.

Priesthood

In the animistic spirit religions, the *shaman* (a medicine man or witch doctor) was believed to have magical powers. Shamans became very important because it was generally believed that they could speak

◀ Sikhism is a religion of India. The Sikh faith was first taught by Guru Nanak (1469–1539). Its symbols include a dagger and a bracelet.

▶ **Christian places of worship come in many shapes and sizes. This unusual building is the chapel of Notre Dame du Haut in France. It was designed by the famous architect Le Corbusier.**

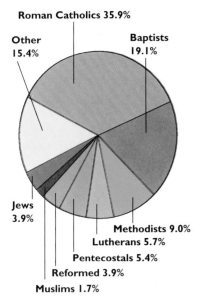

Roman Catholics 35.9%

Other 15.4%

Baptists 19.1%

Jews 3.9%

Methodists 9.0%
Lutherans 5.7%
Pentecostals 5.4%
Reformed 3.9%
Muslims 1.7%

▲ **A pie chart to show the relative sizes of the different religious groups in the United States, expressed in percentages.**

▼ **The holiest place in the Sikh religion is the Golden Temple at Amritsar, India, built in the 1500s.**

directly to the spirits. Even tribal chiefs consulted a shaman before making important decisions.

As civilizations developed, people began to settle in towns and cities. A person often had his or her own house, and so it was felt that the gods should have their own houses, too. Temples, shrines, and holy places were built. The people who dedicated themselves to serving the gods in the temples became known as *priests*. Priests led the prayers, offered the sacrifices, and made sure everyone contributed something to the god. The priests usually lived in the temples, and a high priest headed the religious organization of the community or kingdom.

In many countries, the priests became very powerful because the people believed that the priests'

actions could influence the gods. The priests could also demand temple *stithes*, or taxes, with which to run the temples and at the same time make the gods happy. To keep the priesthood from gaining too much power, many kings made themselves head of the religion. They usually did this either by claiming to be a god or by claiming to be descended from a god. Thus, the king had power over both the religion and the government. The pharaohs of ancient Egypt, the emperors of ancient China, and the Caesars of the Roman Empire are examples of rulers who were considered sacred and who were worshiped as gods.

The priests of modern-day religions are known by various names, such as minister, priest, rabbi, and imam. These religious leaders take charge of teaching their followers about their god and about their god's instructions for people. They conduct religious rituals and celebrations and help people in need.

Rites and Rituals

The rites and rituals of a religion are the ways in which believers show their devotion to a god. There have been thousands of kinds of religious rituals throughout history. They differed according to the event being celebrated, the god being worshiped, and the traditions of the people doing the worshiping.

Most religious rituals center around the important events in life: becoming an adult, marriage, death, harvest, planting time, and so on. All modern-day religions have, or once had, special rituals or ceremonies to celebrate these important occasions.

Many different objects have been used in the performance of rituals. Each object *symbolizes*, or stands for, a certain religious idea or belief. Food (bread and wine) is used in the services of many Christian sects and in the Jewish Passover meal. The Muslims use water to wash their feet

◀ **Muslims worship Allah in mosques. This modern mosque is the Great Mosque at Djenne in Mali, West Africa. It is built of sun-dried mud bricks.**

before entering a mosque. Other religious rites have involved the use of incense, oil, fire, special clothing, dances, music, statues, and many other symbols.

Religious rites and rituals are usually very old. The Christian ritual of communion can be traced back to the last supper Jesus shared with his disciples. The rite of baptism is a very ancient one in many religions, marking the washing away of original sin or the acceptance of the person, especially a newborn child, into the religious community.

The oldest known form of religious ritual was performed by the prehistoric Neanderthal people, who lived from 110,000 until 35,000 years ago. The Neanderthals were the first people known to have buried their dead. They laid the bodies curled up in graves, and placed tools, food, and weapons with the bodies. These burials show that Neanderthal people were concerned about the mystery of death. What happens to a person when he or she dies? The Neanderthals didn't know, but they wanted to be sure the dead had enough provisions to help them get along in their new kind of life. The Neanderthals believed that people continue to live, even though they die. This belief is a basic feature of almost all religions—that after death,

human beings join another world, a world of the spirit, where they have *eternal* (forever) life.

▶▶▶▶ **FIND OUT MORE** ◀◀◀◀
Religions of the World see Buddhism; Christianity; Christian Science; Hinduism; Islam; Judaism; Mormon; Orthodox Church; Protestant Churches; Puritan; Roman Catholic Church; Society of Friends; Taoism; Witchcraft
Religious Holidays see Christmas; Easter; Hanukkah; Passover; Yom Kippur
Religious Leaders see Aquinas, Saint Thomas; Becket, Thomas à; Buddha; Clergy; Confucius; Edward the Confessor; Evangelist; Francis of Assisi; Jesus Christ; Joan of Arc; Luther, Martin; Missionary; More, Sir Thomas; Muhammad; Nicholas, Saint; Prophet; Saint; Smith, Joseph; Wesley, John and Charles; Young, Brigham
Religious Movements see Church and State; Crusades; Jewish History; Protestant Reformation
Religious Places see Catacombs; Cathedral; Ganges River; Jerusalem; Mosque; Pagoda; Palestine; Vatican City; Westminster Abbey
Religious Rites see Burial Customs; Marriage
Religious Traditions and Writings see Bible; Dead Sea Scrolls; Gods and Goddesses; Koran; Mythology

QUIZ
1. What are the three basic kinds of religious belief?
2. Which religion was founded by Muhammad around A.D. 600?
3. Name two Christian sects.
4. What is a *shaman*?
5. What is the name of the sacred book of the Hindus?
(Answers on page 2304)

WHERE TO DISCOVER MORE

Brown, Julie. *How People Worship.* Milwaukee: Gareth Stevens, Inc., 1991.
Morris, Scott, ed. *Religions of the World.* Broomall, Pennsylvania: Chelsea House, 1993.

▲ **Rembrandt painted this self-portrait around 1660.**

▲ *A Girl with a Broom* by **Rembrandt, Andrew Mellon Collection, National Gallery of Art, Washington, D.C.**

REMBRANDT VAN RIJN (1606–1669)

Even a short list of the world's greatest artists would include the name of the great Dutch master Rembrandt van Rijn. The Netherlands of the 1600s produced many great painters, but Rembrandt outshines them all.

Rembrandt was born in 1606 in the town of Leiden, in the Netherlands, the sixth of seven children of a middle-class miller. He must have been an intelligent child, because he was chosen to be sent to the local Latin school. Later, he entered the University of Leiden but left after a short time there to become an artist's apprentice.

He moved between Leiden and Amsterdam, finally opening a studio at the age of 19 in Amsterdam. Rembrandt never studied in Italy, the world center of painting in his time. As far as we know, he never even went there to see the works of Michelangelo, Raphael, and other great artists. However, he studied with teachers who had been abroad. Rembrandt stayed within the borders of his country, working hard all his life, drawing, etching, and painting.

Look at his painting *A Girl with a Broom*. See how a soft light picks her out of the surrounding gloom. This girl, lost in deep thought, leans on her well-used broom. What thoughts are going on behind those dream-filled eyes? The picture makes you wonder. Rembrandt could raise such a question with his portraits.

The girl's face is modeled by light.

See the highlight on the forehead. Notice how her nose fades off into shadow on one side of her face. A special light brings out the red of her hair and the red bodice she is wearing. But all around her—becoming darker at the edge of the canvas—is gloom. This was Rembrandt's way of painting. He was a master of light and shadow—*chiaroscuro*, artists call it.

Rembrandt did many portraits during his lifetime. He painted people of all ages and many occupations. At the times in life when he was poor, he painted members of his family or the servants. The girl in this painting was probably a servant girl. She appears in several of his works done around the year 1650. Rembrandt did many self-portraits from the time he was a young painter until he was a very old man. He had a collection of unusual headdresses and costumes that he would sometimes wear to change his looks when he used himself for a model.

Rembrandt's etchings and drawings were more famous than his paintings during his lifetime. Many of his pictures in all techniques showed scenes from the Bible. In the centuries since he lived, people have come to see the greatness of his paintings. They are among the most prized possessions of art museums.

▶▶▶▶ **FIND OUT MORE** ◀◀◀◀
Dutch and Flemish Art

RENAISSANCE

The word *Renaissance* means "rebirth." This term was first used in the 1400s in Italy, when a great new search for knowledge and an awakening of interest in the arts was taking place. People were rediscovering the glories of ancient Greece and Rome, and they considered this exciting time a rebirth.

The Renaissance brought a new

LEARN BY DOING

Can you see how Rembrandt has used triangles in his composition? See how the arms, the hands, and the head form one triangle. Then, an opposing triangle comes from the angle of the broom, three flashes of red bodice, and the angle of the overturned bucket.

Try drawing a simple portrait of a friend or a member of your family, using triangles in the composition. You will learn some of the problems a portrait painter faces.

spirit of learning to Europe. Printing with movable type was invented in Europe, along with new ways of making paper. America was discovered, and Magellan proved the world was round by sailing around it. A great struggle for religious reform began with the Protestant Reformation. Copernicus and Galileo made discoveries that established astronomy as a new science. Great discoveries were also taking place in art and architecture. Why so many great artists lived at this time is impossible to explain. It was a time of genius when Western art changed from having a spiritual quality to a lifelike quality.

Renaissance art began in the early 1400s in the Italian city of Florence. Some artists and architects set out to create new art. One of the leaders was an architect, Filippo Brunelleschi. It is said that he measured the ruins of old Roman palaces and temples. He did not copy the old buildings, but combined the ancient plans with his own to come up with a new kind of architecture. His architectural ideas were still being used 500 years later. The Pazzi Chapel in Florence is one very famous church that he designed.

Brunelleschi also discovered *perspective*—how to give a three-dimensional look to the flat surface of a painting. Artists began using perspective almost at once. With perspective, they could make objects in a painting look close up or far away. The Florentine artist Masaccio was one of the first artists to use perspective.

Donatello, a great sculptor in Florence during the early Renaissance, had new ideas about sculpture. In his statue of *David*, the slayer of Goliath (shown here), he tried to capture the appearance of a teenage boy. Donatello carefully studied the human form before creating this 5-foot (1.5-m) sculpture.

About the same time as Donatello, another sculptor,

Claus Sluter, was working in the court of the Duke of Burgundy (in what is now France). Sluter also created sculpture that accurately showed the human form.

In the country of Flanders (now in Belgium), a painter named Jan van Eyck was experimenting with oil painting. Painters before van Eyck had used *egg tempera*—powdered paints mixed with egg. Van Eyck was probably the first to use oil. He had found that egg tempera dried too quickly. The slower drying oil paint enabled him to work more slowly and pay attention to detail.

One of van Eyck's masterpieces is the picture shown with the article on MARRIAGE, *Giovanni Arnolfini and His Bride*. The young man and his bride touch hands tenderly as they pose in their new home. The picture was painted in 1434, and in it you can see many details of a home of that time: the chandelier hanging over the young couple, the slippers left carelessly on the floor, even the little family dog! Van Eyck opened a new world of detail that painters continued to *depict* (show) for hundreds of years.

During the 1400s, artists in Italy, Flanders, and elsewhere began to experiment with new methods and styles of painting. The

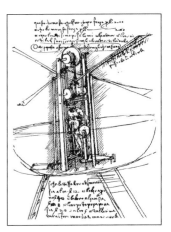

▲ The Tempietto in Rome was built to mark the probable site of St. Peter's crucifixion. Its classical lines show the influence of ancient Greek architecture on Renaissance buildings.

▲ A sketch for a flying machine drawn by Leonardo da Vinci.

◀ A statue of *David* by the sculptor Donatello.

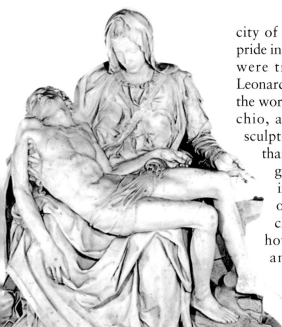

▲ Michelangelo's marble masterpiece, the *Pietà*, depicts Mary holding the dead Jesus just taken down from the cross.

city of Florence took tremendous pride in its artists, and many masters were trained in its workshops. Leonardo da Vinci studied there, in the workshop of Andrea del Verrocchio, a well-known painter and sculptor. Leonardo became more than a master painter. He was a genius who developed amazingly accurate theories in biology, engineering, physics, chemistry, architecture, war, how the human body works, and many other subjects. Leonardo's notebooks and sketches, containing thousands of ideas, questions, and theories that he kept in secret journals, have been saved. One famous illustration is his sketch of a flying machine—a few hundred years ahead of its time.

Michelangelo Buonarroti, born 23 years after Leonardo, was apprenticed to the Florentine painter Domenico Ghirlandaio. While learning from his master, he worked at developing his own style. Michelangelo wanted to know all about the human body in order to draw, paint, and sculpt it accurately. Michelangelo was asked by Pope Julian II to paint

▲ *Madonna and Child and Angels* by the Italian Renaissance painter Botticelli. This work of art shows the warm, gentle beauty of Botticelli's paintings.

▼ Traders like these goldsmiths, and other skilled craftsmen, brought great wealth to the Italian city of Florence during the Renaissance.

frescoes (paintings on damp plaster) for the walls and ceiling of the Sistine Chapel. He spent four years creating this masterpiece, all the time protesting that he was a sculptor, not a painter.

In 1504, a young painter, Raphael (Raffaello Sanzio in Italian), arrived in Florence. He studied the work of Leonardo and Michelangelo, using their techniques to produce his own style. His Madonnas have become particularly famous.

Several other master painters were working at

ideas at last moved across the channel to England, where the Renaissance style in architecture influenced Christopher Wren in his design of St. Paul's Cathedral in London. By 1650, the Renaissance thirst for knowledge and for new ideas and techniques in art and architecture had finally spread throughout Europe.

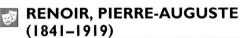

▼ Some people began to think that the prosperity of the Renaissance led to excess. In Florence, a friar named Savonarola led a reaction against materialism. He called people to repent of their sinful lives and had their worldly possessions burned in bonfires.

this time. Titian, Giorgione, Tintoretto, Veronese, and Correggio were among the great painters of the city of Venice. Other artists were Fra Bartolommeo, Fra Filippo Lippi, Fra Angelico, Piero della Francesca, Andrea Mantegna, and Sandro Botticelli.

The influence of Italian Renaissance art spread to other countries. Artists from all over Europe went to Florence, Venice, and other Italian cities to study. France, following the lead of Italy, began training and supporting its own artists late in the 1400s. In the 1600s, the Renaissance came to Spain. In architecture, this brought the building of great cathedrals in that country. Somewhat later, the artists El Greco and Diego Velázquez painted their magnificent works. The Renaissance moved north to Germany and to the Low Countries, where the Flemish and Dutch artists flourished. Renaissance

▶▶▶▶ **FIND OUT MORE** ◀◀◀◀

Architecture; Art History; Baroque Period; El Greco; Giotto Di Bondone; Italian History; Leonardo da Vinci; Michelangelo Buonarroti; Middle Ages; Raphael; Rembrandt van Rijn; Sculpture; Titian

RENOIR, PIERRE-AUGUSTE (1841–1919)

Pierre-Auguste Renoir was one of the leaders of the Impressionists. His paintings were laughed at and rejected for many years. But people came to appreciate the gently rounded forms and the soft, warm colors of the world he painted, and his works became very popular.

Renoir was born in Limoges, France. He grew up in Paris. Renoir liked to call himself a "workman-painter" rather than an artist, because he came from a family of

▲ Angelo Dori, a rich gentleman, is remembered today, because the great artist Raphael painted his portrait.

▲ *Dancing at the Moulin de la Galette* by Pierre-Auguste Renoir.

▲ *Girl with a Straw Hat* by Pierre-Auguste Renoir.

▷ *Asexual reproduction—reproduction with only one parent—is common in small, simple organisms such as the amoeba. To reproduce, the amoeba splits into two by the process of cell division known as* mitosis. *All offspring from asexual reproduction are identical to the parent.*

craftspeople. He was proud to be descended from a shoemaker, a tailor, and a carpenter. He himself became an apprentice porcelain painter at 14, painting designs on fine china. The money he earned at this trade paid for lessons in drawing at the Academy of Fine Arts when he was 21. Several long, hard years of study and work followed. Then Renoir and his friend Claude Monet began working together perfecting the newly discovered way of painting outdoors, with separate touches of vivid color. In 1874, painters using this technique were called "Impressionists." Renoir's painting soon began to attract attention. The outstanding work of this period is *Dancing at the Moulin de la Galette* (pictured here).

When Renoir was 40, he married a 19-year-old girl, Aline Charigot. She was the model for the portrait shown here and for many of Renoir's paintings. He settled down into a happy family life. He continued to experiment with different painting techniques. He kept on painting for the rest of his life. On the day he died, he remarked as he put away his brushes after painting, "I think I am beginning to understand something about it."

▶ ▶ ▶ ▶ **FIND OUT MORE** ◀ ◀ ◀ ◀
Impressionism

REPORTER

SEE JOURNALISM, NEWSPAPER

REPRODUCTION

Reproduction is the way an *organism* (a living plant or animal) produces another organism like itself. All species must reproduce in order to survive. This is done in several different ways.

Reproduction can be *asexual* or *sexual*. In asexual reproduction there is only one parent. In sexual reproduction, there are two parents.

Asexual Reproduction
Many simple plants and animals reproduce asexually. The simplest kind of asexual reproduction is *fission*, or division. The organism splits

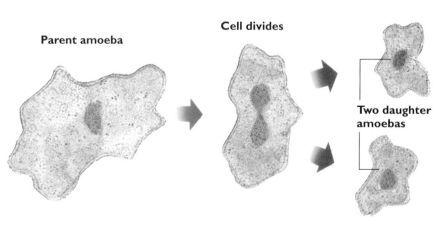

Parent amoeba   Cell divides   Two daughter amoebas

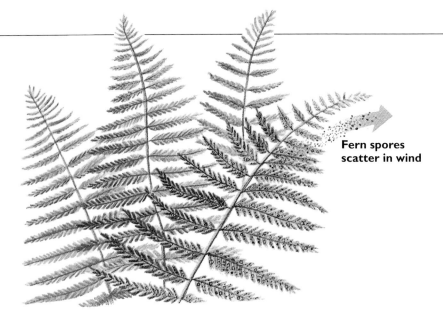

Fern spores scatter in wind

◀ **Ferns reproduce by spores. These are formed in small capsules under the fern's leaves, and are spread by the wind.**

in half, and each half becomes, or is, a separate organism.

Budding is a form of asexual reproduction. The parent organism grows a bump, called a *bud*, which gets bigger and stronger until it is a complete organism able to live by itself. Then it drops off the parent and starts a life of its own. Sometimes the buds do not drop off. They remain together in a collection of organisms called a *colony*. Certain sponges are colonies of organisms formed by budding.

Bacteria, protozoa, and all plants except seed plants reproduce by forming *spores*. These spores, which contain a few cells from the parent, are usually wrapped in a hard, protective coating. A spore may be carried far away by wind or water, and if dropped in a suitable place, it will

begin to divide and develop into a new organism.

Vegetative reproduction is common in plants. Part of the plant sends out roots that grow shoots. Eventually this part produces a complete

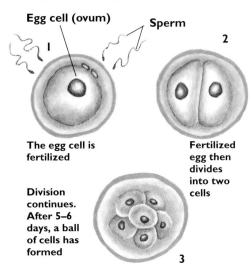

Egg cell (ovum) Sperm

1

The egg cell is fertilized

2

Fertilized egg then divides into two cells

Division continues. After 5–6 days, a ball of cells has formed

3

◀ **(1) When the female egg cell or ovum is fertilized by the male sperm, the nuclei of the two cells merge. (2) The fertilized egg then grows by dividing, (3) creating a ball of cells in five or six days. This continues to divide until a new organism is formed.**

new plant. The part may become separated from the parent plant or it may remain attached to it. Examples of these parts are *bulbs, corms, tubers,* and *rhizomes.*

Sexual Reproduction

In sexual reproduction, a male sex cell, called a *sperm, fertilizes,* or joins with, a female cell, called an *ovum* or egg, to form one fertilized cell. This fertilized cell divides over and over to form a new organism.

The sex cells are produced by sex

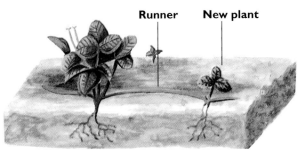

Runner New plant

▲ **Strawberry plants reproduce themselves asexually by means of runners. The new little strawberry plants which are formed at the end of each runner are exact copies of the parent strawberry plant.**

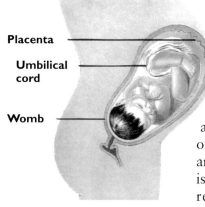

Placenta

Umbilical cord

Womb

▲ A human baby inside its mother's womb or uterus. This is a hollow organ in the mother's abdomen. The baby grows there for nine months. The umbilical cord provides the baby with air and food.

organs in the bodies of the parent organisms. In most animals, the sexes are separated—male animals produce male sex cells, female animals produce female cells. In some animals and in most plants, each organism has both male and female sex organs and, therefore, produces both kinds of sex cells. But even then the male and female cells from the same organism do not usually join together to reproduce. A male cell from one organism fertilizes the female cell of another.

Unlike asexual reproduction, the type that results in offspring identical to the single parent, sexual reproduction produces offspring that share some features of both parents. This is because the mother provides half the information about what the offspring is going to look like, and the father provides the other half. The information is carried by *chromosomes*, tiny threads in the *nucleus* (core) of the sex cells.

Every mature sex cell contains only half as many chromosomes as every body cell. A human body cell contains 23 *pairs* of matched chro-

mosomes, while a human sex cell, male or female, only contains 23 single chromosomes (one of each pair). You might say that a body cell answers every question twice. The body cell has two chromosomes with two *genes* (bits of information) determining, for example, what the eye color is going to be. A sex cell carries only one chromosome with a gene for eye color, so it has only one gene for eye color.

The way in which pairs of chromosomes divide to become single chromosomes is called *meiosis*. In meiosis, the pairs of chromosomes line up opposite each other in the nucleus. Then they separate, one chromosome from each pair going to each end of the nucleus. The nucleus divides in half, forming two nuclei. Each nucleus has one member of each chromosome pair. These nuclei divide again, so that four sex nuclei

▼ From seven to nine months the baby continues to grow and strengthen. Substances are passed from the mother's bloodstream that will help the newborn baby fight disease.

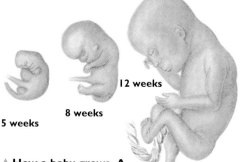

12 weeks

8 weeks

5 weeks

▲ How a baby grows. A human pregnancy usually lasts from 38–40 weeks. At 12 weeks the baby is about 2½ in (9 cm) long and weighs about ½ oz (14 g).

▶ The baby has doubled in size by four months. It has fingers and toes. By seven months, most of the organs of the baby's body, such as its lungs, are working properly. With the help of modern medical techniques, it may be capable of surviving if it is born early.

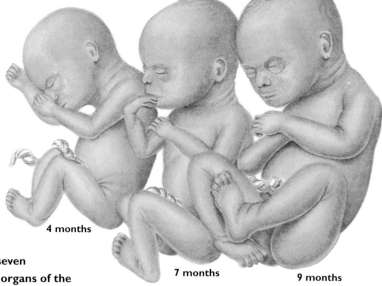

4 months

7 months

9 months

▲ After nine months of growing inside its mother's womb, the baby is fully developed and is ready to be born.

are eventually formed.

When a male sex cell joins with the female sex cell, the chromosomes are brought together in pairs again. One member of each pair comes from each parent. The new cell formed is called a *zygote*. It divides into two cells, then each divides to form four cells. The four divide into eight, and so on. Each of these cells contains the same chromosomes as the zygote. This kind of division, in which both members of each pair of chromosomes are passed on, is *mitosis*.

The divisions happen very quickly, and soon the embryo is a tight ball of cells. Then the cells begin to *differentiate*. If it is an animal embryo, some cells form an outer skin for the embryo; other cells begin to form a stomach; still others form blood and muscle. The study of the development of embryos is called *embryology*.

Fertilization for sexual reproduction takes place in different ways. In flowering plants, both the male sex cells (sperm), and female sex cells (eggs called ova) are produced in the flower. The pollen containing the sperm is formed in the *stamens*. The pollen from one flower is carried to the *pistil* of another by insects, wind, or water. The sperm enter the long stalk of the pistil and fertilize the eggs. The eggs are produced by the *ovary* at the base of the flower. Fertilization results in a seed, a part of which is an embryo. Often the ovary swells up to form a protective fruit. These fruits, with seeds inside, are eaten by birds or other animals. The fruit is digested, but the undigestible seeds pass unharmed through the animal and are expelled. If a seed falls on soil where it can grow, it will send out roots and stems and develop into a new plant.

Many other plants fertilize and reproduce in similar ways. The parts that are found in the flowers of flowering plants are found elsewhere in plants that do not have flowers. Some plants alternate sexual and asexual reproduction. One generation reproduces sexually, the next generation reproduces asexually, and then the next sexually again. Ferns and mosses alternate like this.

In animals, fertilization may be *internal* or *external*. Internal fertilization takes place inside the body of the female. External fertilization takes place outside the body.

In external fertilization, the female lays the eggs and the male fertilizes them after she has laid them. In order for the sperm to penetrate the egg, the egg cannot have a hard shell. An egg without a shell would dry out on land, so external fertilization usually takes place in water. Fish and amphibians (frogs and salamanders) reproduce this way.

In most land animals and birds, fertilization is internal. The male inserts the sperm directly into the female's body, where the sperm unites with the egg to form the embryo. The embryo may then develop externally or internally. In external development, the embryo, together with some food (egg yolk),

HOW LONG SOME ANIMALS TAKE TO DEVELOP
Human being 9 months
Elephant 20–22 months
Honeybee 3 days (from egg to larva)
Salmon 19–80 days, depending on the temperature of the water in which the eggs are laid
Giant salamander 8–12 weeks
Hawk 3–4 weeks
Python about 2 weeks depending on the temperature when the eggs are laid
Dog 8–9 weeks
Cat 9 weeks
Rat 3 weeks
Kangaroo 6 weeks

▼ The reproductive organs of flowering plants are contained within the plant's flower.

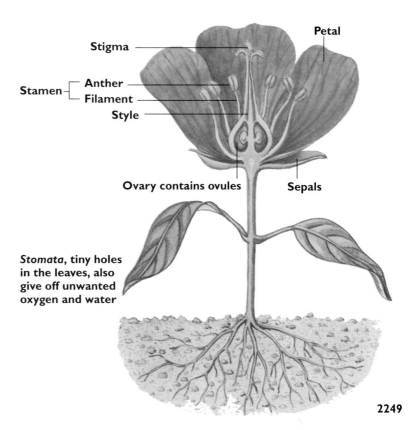

Stigma

Stamen — Anther — Filament

Style

Petal

Ovary contains ovules

Sepals

Stomata, tiny holes in the leaves, also give off unwanted oxygen and water

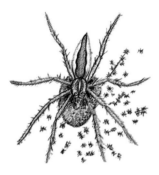

▲ A mother dolphin stays near her baby in order to protect it.

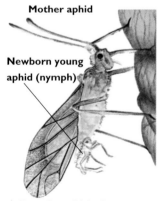

▲ A few insects, like this mother spider, look after their young.

Mother aphid

Newborn young aphid (nymph)

▲ Female aphids do not need to mate with a male in order to produce young. This is an example of *parthenogenesis*.

is covered with a hard shell and is laid as an egg. In internal development, the embryo develops in a womb inside the mother's body.

The number of offspring a mother gives birth to at one time depends on the number of eggs fertilized. In human mothers, only one egg is usually fertilized. If more than one is fertilized, the mother may have a *multiple birth*—twins, triplets, or even more. *Identical twins* are produced when a single fertilized egg divides into two separate cells; these daughter cells contain exactly the same chromosomes and go on to develop into two offspring that are alike in every way.

Animals that take care of their young for a long time after birth usually have only a few offspring at a time. These are often almost helpless at birth. Animals that don't care for their young after birth, such as the green sea turtle, often lay hundreds of eggs. They have to produce so many because only a few survive.

Other Kinds of Reproduction

Sometimes organisms reproduce in ways that cannot easily be called sexual or asexual. One-celled animals such as paramecia may reproduce by *conjugation*. Two animals simply join together and trade *nuclear matter* (matter from the inner core of their cells). Then they separate and each one divides twice to produce four new animals.

Some organisms, such as certain flatworms and jellyfish, can reproduce sexually or asexually. In *parthenogenesis*, an egg that has not been fertilized develops into an embryo and then into a new organism. Bees reproduce this way. An unfertilized egg laid by the queen bee develops into a male drone; a fertilized egg becomes a female worker. A fertilized egg that is fed special food becomes a queen.

▶ ▶ ▶ ▶ **FIND OUT MORE** ◀ ◀ ◀ ◀
Alternation of Generations see
Fern; Mosses and Liverworts
Asexual Reproduction see
Bacteria; Mushroom; Plant Breeding;
Protozoan; Yeast
Genes and Chromosomes see
Cell; Evolution; Genetics
Sexual Reproduction see
Amphibian; Animal families; Australian
Mammals; Egg; Mammal; Marsupial;
Metamorphosis; Plant; Seeds and Fruit

REPTILE

A snake is a *reptile*—a cold-blooded, air-breathing animal with a backbone as well as scales on its skin. Lizards are also reptiles. Snakes and lizards are close relatives and belong to the same *order* (group) of reptiles. Turtles belong to another reptile order, and alligators and crocodiles are members of a third order. The fourth, and last, order of reptiles has only one member—the tuatara, a strange little lizardlike animal that lives on a few islands off New Zealand.

The tuatara has not changed much in 200 million years. It is the closest surviving descendant of the first reptiles, the *cotylosaurs*. Cotylosaurs are called stem reptiles, because all of the other reptiles *stemmed* (branched out) from them. Among the branches were the turtles, the crocodiles, the lizards, and the *therapsids*, the reptiles that gave rise to mammals and the dinosaurs.

The time when the dinosaurs lived is called the age of the reptiles. It fell midway between the age of *amphibians* (animals that live both on land and in water) and the age of mammals. In development, reptiles fall midway between amphibians and mammals and birds. Amphibians gave rise to reptiles, and reptiles gave rise to mammals and birds.

Reptiles inherited the egg from the amphibians. But the reptiles greatly

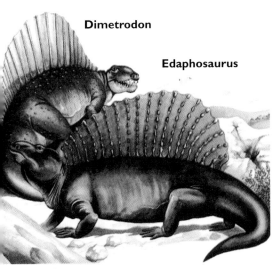

Dimetrodon

Edaphosaurus

▲ Examples of primitive reptiles that lived more than 250 million years ago. The "sails" on their backs were bony spines covered with skin. These were used to help control the reptiles' body heat. When sideways to the sun's rays, they absorbed heat, and when facing away from the sun, they released it.

improved the amphibian egg. They made it watertight, not to keep water out but to keep juices in. Amphibians had to lay their eggs in water to keep them from drying out. Reptiles could lay their eggs on land. This allowed them to become the first true land animals. Some reptiles have gone even further, giving birth to live young. This characteristic was passed on to the mammals, while egg-laying was passed on to the birds.

Reptiles are often said to be "cold-blooded," like the amphibians, as opposed to "warm-blooded," like birds and mammals. This does not mean that their blood is always cold. It just means that their temperature changes with the temperature of their surroundings. If a reptile lives in a warm place and stays active, its temperature may be higher than that of many warm-blooded animals.

Reptile Orders

The turtle developed in the age of the dinosaurs and has not changed very much since then. It has not changed, because armor has enabled it to survive without changing. Every turtle has some sort of shell. In some turtles, the shell is only a thick, leathery skin, but in most turtles, it is a double layer of hard, horny scales and tightly fitted bones.

The shell is wonderful for protection, but it is not so good for other things. In order to walk, every turtle has to slide its shoulders back into its rib cage. In order to breathe, it has to rearrange its insides. Getting the head into the shell is a problem. Most turtles curl their necks up into an S-shape.

The crocodilians—including crocodiles and alligators—are almost as old as the turtle. And although their species is very

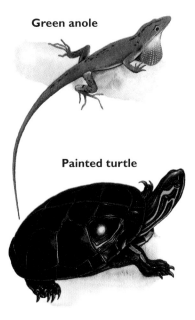

Green anole

Painted turtle

▲ The green anole is sometimes called the "American chameleon," because it can change color. The painted turtle is a freshwater turtle that lives in shallow lakes and streams.

▲ Geckos are small lizards that live in hot climates. They are often found inside houses. The suckerlike pads on their feet enable them to run across the ceiling when they are hunting insects.

▼ Chameleons are insectivorous reptiles. They catch insects with their long, sticky tongues. They can change the color of their skins by hormone activity. Color changes are triggered by changes in their surroundings or by fright or anger.

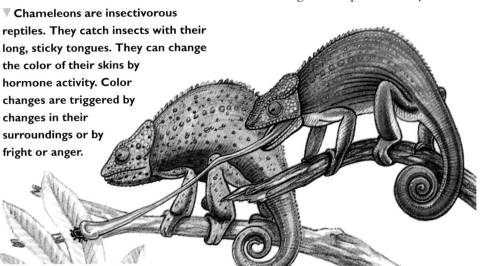

▲ Two large crocodiles bask in the sun on a riverbank. They do this to regulate their body temperature.

WHERE TO DISCOVER MORE

Scott, Jack Denton. *Alligator.* New York: Putnam, 1984.

Simon, Seymour. *Poisonous Snakes.* New York: Four Winds Press, 1981.

► Poisonous snakes like the king cobra inject venom by biting victims with their fangs.

old, crocodiles and alligators are very modern in some ways. They are the only reptiles with four-chambered hearts, like a human heart. Crocodiles and alligators may live to be more than 50 years old and grow to 20 feet (6 m) long. Like most reptiles, they eat meat. Occasionally a crocodile or an alligator may attack a human being.

Lizards and snakes are the most prevalent reptiles. Of the approximately 6,000 different *species* (kinds), there are slightly more kinds of lizards than snakes. A couple of species of snakes have tiny *vestigial* (leftover, almost useless) legs, and a few kinds of lizards are legless. But all lizards have eyelids, and no snakes have eyelids. A snake's eyes are always open. The scales on a lizard's skin are about the same all over,

▲The brightly colored eastern fence lizard is related to the iguana.

while a snake usually has a special row of wide, flat scales on its belly. The snake can grip the ground with these scales to move itself about. Lizards have outside ears, and snakes do not. Most lizards can drop off their tails for protection and grow new ones. Snakes cannot do this.

King cobra

▶ ▶ ▶ ▶ **FIND OUT MORE** ◀ ◀ ◀ ◀
Individual Reptiles see Alligators and Crocodiles; Lizard; Snake; Turtle
Reptile Characteristics see Animal Defenses; Animal Movement; Egg; Molting; Regeneration; Reproduction; Respiration; Vertebrate
Reptile Evolution see Amphibian; Birds of the Past; Dinosaur; Evolution; Fossil; Mammal; Rare Animal

REPUBLIC

A nation that does not have a king or queen or some other monarch as leader of the government is called a *republic*. A monarch inherits his or her position as head of the government, but the leader of a republic comes to power through other means.

Most modern republics have come into being as the result of revolution and the overthrow of a monarch. The 13 colonies of North America were ruled by the British monarch until 1776. During the Revolutionary War, the colonies overthrew British monarchical rule and established a republic, a form of government in which its president and lawmakers were elected by the people. In 1789, the French people overthrew their monarch and set up a republic. By the 1940s, the United Kingdom, the Dutch, and the Scandinavian monarchies were the only nonrepublican governments in Europe.

The word "republic" is often confused with "democracy." A republic can be a democracy when the people directly elect the officials of the government, and when these elected officials follow the will of the people. But a republic can also be a dictatorship in which top officials are not elected by the people directly, or in which the officials do not follow the will of the people.

The earliest republics known in detail are the city-states of ancient Greece. Except for slaves, each male citizen had a vote. The ancient Romans also formed a republic that lasted until 27 B.C., after which Rome became a monarchy run by emperors. The word *republic* comes from the Latin term *res publica*, meaning "public affair." The oldest existing republic is probably the tiny country of San Marino (located in Italy, north of Rome). It was founded as a republic in the 300s. Switzerland organized as a republic in 1291. With few exceptions, most countries today have republican governments.

▶▶▶▶ **FIND OUT MORE** ◀◀◀◀
Democracy; Government; Greece, Ancient; Nation; Revolution; Revolutionary War; Rome, Ancient

◀ The Roman senate was a council of elders who advised the *consuls*, the two chief officials of the Roman republic. As time went by, the senate's powers increased until it became the chief governing body of the republic. When Rome ceased to be a republic, the senate lost some of its powers, but it continued to play an important part in government. The senate house was called the *curia*.

A person at rest breathes in and out some 13 times a minute. With each breath, about 30 cubic inches (500 cc) of air is taken in.

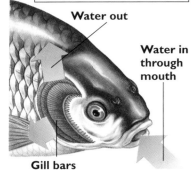

Water out

Water in through mouth

Gill bars

▲ Like almost all living things, fish need oxygen. They are able to breathe it from the water by means of gills. When the fish takes in water through its mouth, the water passes across the gills before being passed out of the fish again. The water contains dissolved oxygen, which is absorbed by the blood in the fish's gills.

▶ Mammals breathe with their lungs. Air is taken in through the nose and mouth and carried to the lungs down the *trachea,* or windpipe. The lungs have millions of tiny air sacks called *alveoli.* Oxygen is brought to them from the windpipe through branching air tubes: the *bronchi* and *bronchioles.* It passes through the walls of the alveoli and into blood vessels on the other side, which carry oxygen around the body. When breathing, the movements of the chest and abdominal muscles suck air into the lungs for oxygen and blow out carbon dioxide.

2254

RESERVOIR

SEE WATER SUPPLY

RESIN

SEE SYNTHETICS

RESONANCE

SEE SOUND

RESPIRATION

All living things must have energy. They obtain this energy through *respiration,* a process that changes food to energy. Most living things use *oxygen* in respiration. Oxygen is an element (basic chemical substance) that combines very readily with other elements in a process called *oxidation.* Burning is a kind of oxidation, and rusting is another kind. In oxidation, new chemical *compounds* (combina-

Water vapor out   **Carbon dioxide in**

Oxygen out

▲ Plants "breathe" through their leaves. The plant needs carbon dioxide to make its food. It takes this in from the air through tiny holes in the leaf called *stomata* and gives out oxygen in return.

tions) are formed and energy is produced.

Most living things get their oxygen from the air or from the water. The oxygen passes to the cells where it is used to *oxidize* (burn) food. Oxidation produces energy, carbon dioxide, and water. The energy is used for the work and growth of the cell. The carbon dioxide and water are given off as waste.

Simple animals have no trouble obtaining oxygen. Their cells *absorb* (soak up) oxygen directly from the air or water they live in. But in larger animals only a few cells are in direct contact with air or water. Most of their cells are buried deep within their bodies, and oxygen must reach them through a respiratory system. The respiratory

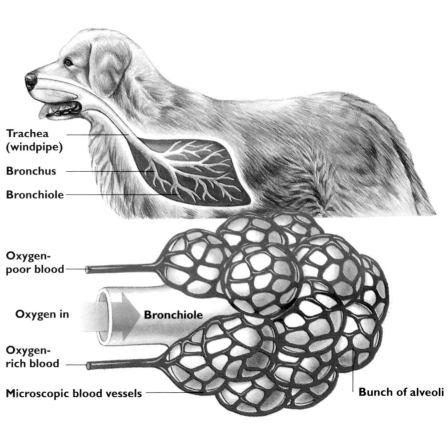

Trachea (windpipe)

Bronchus

Bronchiole

Oxygen-poor blood

Oxygen in   **Bronchiole**

Oxygen-rich blood

Microscopic blood vessels   **Bunch of alveoli**

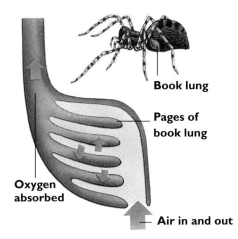

▲ Some spiders have respiratory systems called "book" lungs. These have a large surface area, which is arranged rather like the pages of a book, to help the spider absorb the maximum amount of oxygen.

systems of many animals are composed of *respiratory organs* that pick up oxygen from their surroundings. These respiratory organs have thin, wet walls and a substantial blood supply. The *gills* of a fish pick up oxygen from water. The *lungs* of human beings and other land animals pick up oxygen from the air. The oxygen then passes through the thin walls of the respiratory organ into the blood, where it combines with the red blood cells. The blood carries the oxygen through smaller and smaller blood vessels until it reaches the thin-walled vessels called *capillaries*. The oxygen passes through the walls of the capillaries and into the cells, where oxidation takes place. The waste carbon dioxide and water given off by oxidation go back into the blood and are carried to the respiratory organ.

In the respiratory organ, the blood cells give off the carbon dioxide and water and pick up fresh oxygen. The carbon dioxide and water leave the body. When you breathe in, you bring oxygen in the air into your body. When you breathe out, you are forcing out carbon dioxide and water, in the form of vapor.

The blood of insects does not carry oxygen. Oxygen enters the body through small openings, called *spiracles,* and passes into tubes called *tracheae.* The trachea carry the oxygen to all parts of the body.

▶ ▶ ▶ ▶ **FIND OUT MORE** ◀ ◀ ◀ ◀
Artificial Respiration; Blood; Breathing; Digestion; Nose

RESTAURANT

Restaurants prepare and sell food and drink. There are many types of restaurants, including cafeterias, ice-cream parlors, coffeehouses, tea-rooms, roadside and fast-food restaurants, and restaurants that specialize in the food of one particular country. Some restaurants offer a *menu* (list of foods served) of hot-dogs and hamburgers at an average cost of less than $4. Others offer a variety of full meals prepared to delight the most particular diner, at a much higher price.

The type of service that customers receive depends on the kind of restaurant they are in. Customers in cafeterias (similar to the one that may be in your school) see the available food and choose what they please. They may serve themselves (buffet-style) or be served by waiters and waitresses. In most restaurants, customers are seated, and the food they select from the menu is brought to them.

In ancient times, people thought that a person's breath was actually the life spirit. The word *inspiration* comes from two Latin words meaning "to breathe into." So when you are inspired, something has put breath—or spirit and life—into you.

▼ There are many different types of restaurants all over the world that serve food to cater to the tastes of people of various nationalities.

It is impossible to state which was the first restaurant in the world, but one of the earliest bearing that name was opened in Madrid, Spain, in the 1720s. One of its dishwashers was the famous Spanish painter Goya! Restaurants located at the highest points in the world include those built at the top of ski lift stations at mountain ski resorts.

A restaurant owner must have a large staff to run the business efficiently. The headwaiter or hostess seats customers and may take their orders. Waiters serve the food, and busboys set and clear the tables. The *chef* (head cook) and other cooks prepare the meals. (The chef sometimes plans the menu as well.) Dishwashers and janitors are necessary, too.

Eating out has not always been as popular as it is today. Before the 1800s, people almost always had their meals at home. They ate at inns, taverns, and other restaurants only when they were traveling. Many taverns and coffeehouses were also popular meeting places for writers, politicians, and people who just wanted an evening out.

Early restaurants served only one kind of meal, at one price, and at a certain time. The meal was known by the French words *table d'hôte*, meaning "table of the host." This expression is still used to mean a full meal (appetizer, main course, and dessert) served at a fixed price. French restaurants added the custom of serving meals *a la carte*, meaning "by the menu." Customers were given a list of the foods that were available, and they could make their choice. The first American restaurant (separate from a hotel) was Delmonico's, which opened in 1827 in New York City.

As towns and cities grew, so did the need for more restaurants. Many people could no longer get home easily for lunch. In the late 1800s, a new kind of self-service restaurant—the cafeteria—was opened. At first, there were separate cafeterias for men and women. In the 1900s, cafeterias became very popular. Today, as more and more people travel by automobile, roadside, carry-out, and fast-food restaurants have been opened to meet their needs.

▶▶▶▶ **FIND OUT MORE** ◀◀◀◀
Food; Hotels and Motels

REVERE, PAUL (1735–1818)

"Listen, my children, and you shall hear
Of the midnight ride of Paul Revere . . ."

You may have heard these famous lines of poetry by Henry Wadsworth Longfellow about one of the heroes of the Revolutionary War. Paul Revere was a Boston silversmith and patriot. He is remembered for his brave ride through the Massachusetts countryside to warn the farmers that British troops were coming.

▲ **Paul Revere on his heroic ride to Lexington and Concord to warn the people of the approach of the British troops. Although Revere was captured, his mission was successful and his bravery has never been forgotten.**

Revere was born in Boston, Massachusetts. He was the third of 12 children of a silversmith. Paul learned the trade from his father and became a master craftsman. Many of the fine silver pieces he designed are exhibited in many museums today. Revere also cast bells and made cannons in his foundry. He produced bolts, spikes, pumps, and copper

Later in life, Paul Revere was successful in various business enterprises, including shipping ice to the West Indies.

parts for the ship *Old Ironsides*. He designed the first issue of Continental money and the seal of the state of Massachusetts, which the state still uses today.

Revere was an active patriot. He donned war paint and feathers to take part in the Boston Tea Party. He often served as a messenger for revolutionary colonial organizations. On the night of April 18, 1775, Revere learned that the British planned to attack Lexington and Concord. He arranged a signal to warn of the British secret move: If they moved by land, one lantern would be hung in the steeple of Boston's Old North Church; if by sea, two lanterns would be hung.

When Revere learned that the British were coming by sea, he gave the signal. Then he rode toward Concord with William Dawes and Samuel Prescott. The three were stopped by a British patrol. Revere was captured and Dawes escaped. Only Prescott rode on to warn Concord. Revere was released later that night. He is believed to have been in Lexington just in time to hear the first shots of the revolution fired.

▶▶▶▶ **FIND OUT MORE** ◀◀◀◀
Boston Tea Party; Longfellow, Henry Wadsworth; Revolutionary War

REVOLUTION

A *revolution* is a method of overthrowing an old system of government and establishing a new one, giving power to those who have overthrown the old order. Revolutions have occurred throughout history for many reasons. A revolution is usually begun when many people in a country become unhappy with the way the country is being run. The government may be too strict with its citizens. It may tax them too heavily. Its laws may be unfair to many. A

▲ In 1848, revolutionaries in France overthrew the restored monarchy and declared a republic. They stormed government buildings in Paris demanding "Bread or death."

strong person, or group of persons, may lead other dissatisfied people toward revolution. When the people think they have enough power, they try to take over the government. Some revolutions have been long and bloody, lasting many years. Others have involved little bloodshed. Sometimes, after a revolution has been successful, another group rises up against it. This movement is called a *counterrevolution*.

The Revolutionary War began because many of the British colonies in North America wanted to separate from England. They resented being governed from abroad and paying unfair taxes. In 1775, they went to war with England. After six years of fighting, the colonies won their independence, and the United States was born. The French Revolution was brought about by the royal family's unjust rule. Most of the people lived in poverty. The people rose against the monarchy and the wealthy ruling class. The king, queen, and many of the nobility were beheaded. In October 1911, the Chinese Revolution began. It was led by Sun Yat-sen against the ruling Manchu *dynasty* (line of royalty). China then became a republic. The Russian Revolution began in 1917 and led to the establishment of a Communist government. Russia became the Union of Soviet Socialist Republics. Soviet

▲ In 1824, Simón Bolívar freed Peru from Spanish rule, when his troops defeated the Spanish forces at the battle of Ayacucho.

▼ The signing of the Declaration of Independence on July 4, 1776, was the major highlight of the Revolution and the birth of a new nation. This is a detail from the painting *The Declaration of Independence* by the artist John Trumbull.

troops put down the Hungarian Revolution of 1956. In the 1959 Cuban Revolution, Fidel Castro came to power. Iran's 1979 revolution ended the shah's rule. In 1986, a rebellion overthrew president Ferdinand Marcos of the Philippines, ending a 20-year dictatorship there. In the early 1990s, many Eastern European countries, East Germany, and Soviet states had gradual revolutions. They rejected Communism and became independent nations.

A *coup d'état* is a kind of revolution in which one group, usually the military, overthrows the constitutional government.

▶ ▶ ▶ ▶ **FIND OUT MORE** ◀ ◀ ◀ ◀
Castro, Fidel; French Revolution; Iran; Revolutionary War; Russian History; Sun Yat-sen

REVOLUTIONARY WAR

"These United Colonies are, and of right ought to be Free and Independent States." So said the Second Continental Congress in the Declaration of Independence in 1776. Many events happened before the colonists were ready to take this stand. It took a long and hard struggle to make these words come true.

The British won the French and Indian War in 1763. They needed money to pay for the war and govern Canada and the eastern Mississippi Valley, which they had taken from the French. Parliament decided to raise funds by increasing taxes in the American colonies. The Stamp Act of 1765 required that tax stamps had to be bought for wills, deeds, and other legal documents. Every newspaper, magazine, almanac, or calendar sold in the colonies also had to be stamped. Americans were not allowed to have anyone *represent* (speak and vote for) them when tax laws were made in Parliament. "No taxation without representation" was the cry of the angry colonists. They wanted the right to help make their own laws, not to be ruled by the Parliament in Britain.

Trouble in Boston
Another act of Parliament that the colonists hated was the Quartering Act. The colonies had to provide

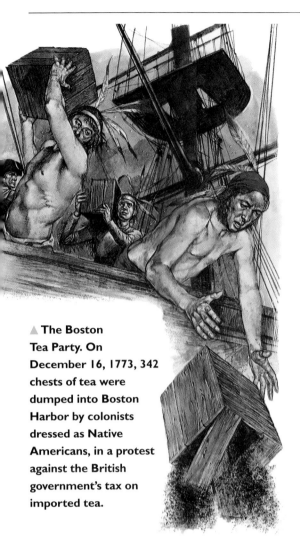

▲ The Boston Tea Party. On December 16, 1773, 342 chests of tea were dumped into Boston Harbor by colonists dressed as Native Americans, in a protest against the British government's tax on imported tea.

were not allowed to vote on the tax. The protest known as the *Boston Tea Party* was held when the ships arrived in Boston Harbor with their cargo. Colonists disguised as Native Americans dumped 342 chests of tea into the harbor. The British promptly closed the harbor. The British governor sailed home, leaving General Thomas Gage in command. The Quartering Act, which had been stopped, was started again. Furthermore, if a British official were charged with a crime against a colonist, he was not tried locally, but sent to Britain for trial.

The people of Boston and of Massachusetts were angry. So were many other colonists. The First Continental Congress met in Philadelphia in September 1774. Every colony except Georgia was represented. The Congress formed the Continental Association, adopted a declaration of rights, and decided not to import British

▼ A map to show the sites of the major battles of the Revolutionary War.

housing and supplies for British soldiers in America. The people of Boston and New York, where many troops were stationed, were especially upset by this law. A noisy crowd of men and boys gathered near Boston's Custom House on a cold March day in 1770. Some of the boys threw snowballs at a British sentry. The sentry called for other soldiers, and the crowd became angrier and angrier. Shots rang out. Three Americans lay dead and eight were wounded (two of the wounded died later). Crispus Attucks, a leader of the crowd and probably a runaway slave, was the first to die. This incident was called the *Boston Massacre*.

The Boston colonists were spurred to violence again three years later, in December of 1773. The British taxed the tea they shipped to America. The tea tax was small, but the colonists

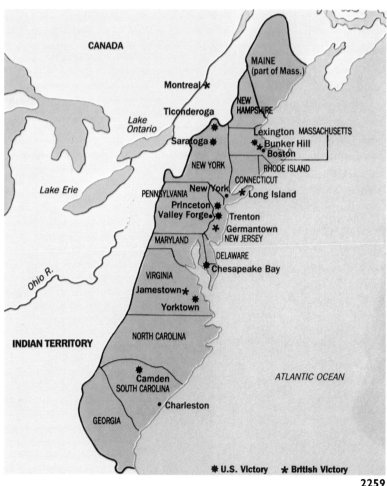

The Bedford Flag, flown on the first day of the revolution, 1775.

The pine tree flag

The Continental Colors

The First Stars and Stripes

▲ Revolutionary War flags.

When the original 13 colonies declared their independence in 1776, the United States was only a fourth of its present size. By 1850, it was a nation of 31 states stretching from the Atlantic to the Pacific, an area of 3 million square miles (8 million sq. km).

goods. The delegates agreed to meet again the following May if Parliament did not rewrite the unjust laws.

The Shot Heard 'Round the World

In April 1775, General Gage marched his British troops from Boston, through Lexington to Concord. Spies had told the British commander that guns and ammunition were stored in Concord. These spies also told Gage that two patriot leaders, Samuel Adams and John Hancock, were hiding in Lexington. Gage planned to

capture the supplies and the rebels. But the Americans also had spies. When the red-coated British started their "secret" march, two Americans saddled their horses and sped through the darkness to warn the colonists at Lexington and Concord that the British were coming.

Those heroic riders were Paul Revere and William Dawes. They were aided by Dr. Samuel Prescott, who took the warning to Concord after Revere was captured.

Gage's 700 or 800 redcoats met a band of *Minutemen* (farmers and shopkeepers who were ready to fight at a minute's notice) lined up on Lexington's village green. No one knows who fired the first shot. But, in the shooting that followed, eight Americans were killed and the rest scattered. The British marched on to Concord. British troops did not find Adams, Hancock, or the supplies, because Dr. Prescott had warned the colonists in Concord.

The British dumped several barrels of flour and set fire to some buildings at Concord before starting back to Boston. The redcoats found their return route blocked by angry Min-

▶ The Battle of Lexington, 1775. British troops fire their muskets at the fleeing Lexington militia.

utemen. Aroused by the news of the Americans killed at Lexington, hundreds of farmers and merchants swarmed toward Concord. The British were able to fight off an attack on Concord's North Bridge. But their return march became a nightmarish retreat. Rifles and muskets were fired from behind every stone wall, building, or brush pile that could hide a Minuteman. By the time the redcoats finally reached the safety of their barracks, 273 of their soldiers had been killed or wounded.

One month later, Ethan Allen and Benedict Arnold led the Green Mountain Boys in the capture of Fort Ticonderoga, the most important British fortress north of the Hudson River. News of their daring attack encouraged the delegates to the Second Continental Congress in Philadelphia. The Congress now had to deal with a real war, so they called for a real army. The Congress chose a wealthy planter from Virginia to command this Continental Army. They felt he was well suited for the job. He had been a lieutenant colonel in Britain's wars with France, and he later led several companies of Virginia volunteer soldiers. His name was George Washington.

The first major battle of the war—the Battle of Bunker Hill—was fought on June 17, 1775. It actually took place on nearby Breed's Hill. The British successfully captured the hill, but more than twice as many British soldiers were killed or wounded as Americans. Many American colonists, called *Loyalists,* were still against breaking away from Britain, even though bat-

◀ **A British grenadier. The British troops, trained for European wars, found fighting in America very different.**

▶ **A Revolutionary War soldier. The Americans were skilled marksmen because of their frontier experience.**

tles had been fought and men killed. This deep-seated struggle between American Patriots and Loyalists went on throughout the Revolution.

The Declaration Leads to Full-Scale War

The Continental Congress continued to hope until the summer of 1776 that Great Britain would be fair to the colonies. Then a delegate from Virginia finally offered a resolution for full independence. Thomas Jefferson wrote the first draft of the document that declared the colonies were free. John Adams and Benjamin Franklin made small changes to the document. Other minor changes were made by the Congress. The Declaration of Independence was approved in Philadelphia, on July 4, 1776.

> The chief weapon used in the Revolutionary War was the flintlock musket with a bayonet. Each soldier carried cartridges of paper, lead bats, and black powder in a box slung over his shoulder.

▼ **The Battle of Bunker Hill was one of the first battles of the war. During this fight, when ammunition was scarce, the American colonel William Prescott told his skilled marksmen, "Don't shoot until you see the whites of their eyes."**

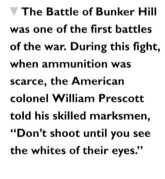

▲ **On Christmas night 1776, George Washington and his men crossed the Delaware River to attack Hessian soldiers at Trenton, New Jersey.**

The Liberty Bell in Philadelphia has become a symbol of American independence. The bell was rung on July 8, 1776, when the Declaration of Independence was read to the cheering crowd that gathered outside Independence Hall.

▶ **American commander John Paul Jones lashed his flagship *Bon Homme Richard* to the British warship *Serapis* and forced its surrender after three hours of bloody fighting.**

That summer, the British shifted the fighting from Boston to New York. Washington's army was pushed from Long Island and Manhattan by troops led by Sir William Howe. Washington was forced to retreat into New Jersey and then into Pennsylvania. Washington and his men crossed the ice-packed Delaware River on Christmas night 1776 in open boats and captured the garrison at Trenton, New Jersey. The troops at Trenton were German soldiers, called *Hessians,* whom the British paid to fight for them. The Americans won a small victory a few days later at Princeton, New Jersey. The British then began a major attempt to capture Philadelphia, the colonial capital. Philadelphia was taken from American hands in the fall of 1777. This was a staggering blow. The Continental Congress moved the capital to York, Pennsylvania, 80 miles (129 km) west of Philadelphia.

The Tide Turns

The British tried to cut the colonies in half by advancing south from Canada with another army commanded by General John Burgoyne. But they were forced to surrender at the Battle of Saratoga in New York. This American victory was the turning point of the war. The French became allies of the Americans after Saratoga. French soldiers, ships, and money aided the American cause. Spain also helped, and the Netherlands loaned money for the fight.

But the American cause was in danger during the dreadful winter of 1777–1778. The British held Philadelphia. The government was in exile at York. And General Washington was camped in the snow at Valley Forge. His men were starving and frozen. The young French nobleman the Marquis de Lafayette was barely 20 when he joined General Washington and spent that winter at Valley Forge. Lafayette did not believe that men could survive such misery and hardship. Washington stated in one report that his 3,000 men could not fight because they had no shoes or warm clothing.

Baron von Steuben, a friend of Benjamin Franklin, brought hope and encouragement to the Americans in the spring of 1778. Von Steuben, a former Prussian (German) officer, trained the Continental soldiers until

they became better fighters, both in groups and as individuals.

The American Navy had had only four ships when the Revolution began. Congress later had more built. Many small, privately owned ships were used as *privateers*, seizing British supply and merchant ships and transporting arms from France. In 1779, John Paul Jones, with his ship, *Bon Homme Richard*, captured the British warship *Serapis* in a spectacular battle.

George Rogers Clark of Virginia captured several British forts in the region of Illinois and Michigan in 1778 and 1779. Clark's victories over the British and their Native American allies helped the Americans gain more favorable terms when the peace treaty was signed. Britain was forced to give all lands east of the Mississippi River to the Americans.

The British turned their efforts to the southern colonies in 1780 and 1781. They captured Savannah, Georgia, and won at Charleston, South Carolina. But they lost at Kings Mountain and Cowpens. American heroes of the South included Francis Marion, the "Swamp Fox," whose guerrillalike (hit-and-run) warfare confused the British troops and led to their defeat.

Surrender at Yorktown

Lord Cornwallis marched his British troops north and occupied Yorktown, Virginia, in midsummer of 1781. He wanted to help the Royal Navy control Virginia, Maryland, and the Chesapeake Bay. General Washington and the French leader, Count Rochambeau, cornered the British troops with the help of Lafayette and General "Mad Anthony" Wayne. The French navy, led by Admiral de Grasse, blocked escape by sea. Lord Cornwallis surrendered at Yorktown on October 17, 1781.

John Adams, Benjamin Franklin, and John Jay started peace talks for the Americans in April 1782. When the Treaty of Paris was signed in September 1783, Great Britain granted independence to the Americans and recognized the new United States of America as a seperate nation.

▶ ▶ ▶ ▶ **FIND OUT MORE** ◀ ◀ ◀ ◀

Background see American Colonies; Boston Massacre; Boston Tea Party; Continental Congress; Declaration of Independence; French and Indian War

Leaders for Independence see Adams, Samuel; Franklin, Benjamin; Hancock, John; Henry, Patrick; Jefferson, Thomas; Paine, Thomas; Revere, Paul

Leaders in War see Allen, Ethan; Clark, George Rogers; Hale, Nathan; Jones, John Paul; Lafayette, Marquis de; Marion, Francis; Washington, George

It has been estimated that the Revolutionary War cost the United States about $100 million.

WHERE TO DISCOVER MORE

Smith, Carter, Ed. *The Revolutionary War: A Sourcebook on Colonial America*. Brookfield, CT: Millbrook Press. 1991.

Meltzer, Milton, Ed. *The American Revolutionaries: A History in Their Own Words 1750–1800*. New York: Crowell, 1987.

◀ Supported by the French, Washington's American army compelled the British forces of Cornwallis to surrender at Yorktown, Virginia, in October 1781. The peace treaty was signed in 1783.

▲ *George Hare*, a portrait by Joshua Reynolds.

 REYNOLDS, JOSHUA (1723–1792)

Joshua Reynolds was the first of several great English portrait painters. He was born in Plympton, in the county of Devon, England. When he was 26, he traveled to Italy, where he studied for two years and saw the works of the great Italian masters.

He returned to London and became a portrait painter, which was the only kind of painter in great demand in England at that time. He painted portraits of many British political and artistic leaders. Reynolds tried to get to know the people whose portraits he painted. He did not just copy faces and costumes. In some way, Reynolds wanted to bring out each sitter's personality and make it come alive on his canvas.

What can you tell about the personality of little George Hare in the portrait shown here? Little boys wore dresses in those days, and George's has fallen down over one shoulder. Reynolds may be saying that George is an active boy who would rather be playing than sitting for his portrait.

▶ *Lord Heathfield* (detail), a portrait by Joshua Reynolds. It was painted to commemorate Lord Heathfield's defense of Gibraltar during a long siege, and conveys the strength and character of its subject.

Why do you suppose George is pointing off into the distance? The pointing finger tends to make your eye follow it out of the picture. Reynolds cleverly balanced that arm with the fallen down sleeve on the opposite side of the picture. The horizontal sash also helps pull your eye back into the picture.

Reynolds was a master of composition. He often experimented with new kinds of paint, and this may be the reason that many of his paintings have deteriorated over the years. He was also a famous teacher of the principles of art.

▶▶▶▶ **FIND OUT MORE** ◀◀◀◀
Art History; Painting; Portrait

 RHINE RIVER

The Rhine is one of the major rivers of Europe. It begins in the Alps Mountains of Switzerland. The river then flows northward for about 820 miles (1,320 km) through Switzerland, Liechtenstein, Austria, Germany, France, and the Netherlands. At Rotterdam in the Netherlands, the Rhine empties into the North Sea. (See the map with the article on EUROPE.)

The Rhine River is an important transportation route in Europe. It is navigable by oceangoing ships as far as Mannheim, Germany, and by river barges as far as Basel, Switzerland. Raw materials, such as oil, are transported up the Rhine River to industrial areas, such as the Ruhr in Germany. Many Swiss and German manufactured goods are carried down the Rhine for export abroad.

South of the German city of Bonn, the Rhine flows through a rugged valley. Grapes grown on the steep hillsides produce the famous Rhine wines. This area is the legendary home of the *Lorelei,* a beautiful Rhine maiden whose singing lured sailors to their death. Many pic-

▶ **Barges travel down the Rhine River in Germany, past lovely towns and castles, green fields, and vineyards.**

turesque castles look down on the Rhine. The castles date from times when riders who lived along the river levied tolls on passing ships. Today, ships sail free of charge. In 1986, the river suffered serious pollution from spilled chemicals.

▶▶▶▶ **FIND OUT MORE** ◀◀◀◀
Germany; Pollution

RHINOCEROS

The rhinoceros is a large, heavy mammal with a thick, loose skin. Rhinoceroses have long bodies and heads but rather short legs. They weigh from 2,000 to 8,000 pounds (900 to 3,600 kg) and have one or two horns above the snout. The two African species have two horns. Three other species—two with one horn and one with two horns—live in parts of Asia. These horns, made up of hairs stuck solidly together, can be very dangerous. But the rhinoceros's primary method of attack is charging.

▶ **The black rhinoceros of Africa is gray rather than black. It has a pointed snout and a hooked upper lip, which helps it grasp leaves when grazing on the bushes it feeds from.**

◀ **The white rhinoceros is another African species. Larger than the black rhino, it is one of the world's biggest land mammals. White rhinos have wide snouts and graze on grassland, where they live in small herds. They have very poor eyesight, but acute hearing and an excellent sense of smell. White rhinos are now rare because they have been hunted almost to extinction for their horns.**

▲ **A male rhinoceros marks his territory with a pile of dung.**

The longest horn on a white rhinoceros measured more than 5 feet (158 cm). It is thought that explorers' reports of beasts like this led to the myth of the unicorn.

In spite of its size, the usually peaceful rhinoceros can charge rapidly when it senses danger. Its eyesight is poor, but its hearing and sense of smell are very keen.

Rhinoceroses are *herbivorous*— they eat grass and other plants. Rhinoceroses spend some of their time in water. They also wallow in the mud to get rid of insect parasites in their skin. A rhinoceros is most active in the morning and at night, when the weather is cool. It spends most of the day resting in the shade. It lives in grassy, marshy areas or in jungles. The rhinoceros usually lives alone, except during the breeding season. The female gives birth to one calf, which she nurses for about two years.

▶▶▶▶ **FIND OUT MORE** ◀◀◀◀
Hoofed Animals;
Horns and Antlers; Mammal

RHODE ISLAND

Which state in the union has the longest name? The state with the smallest area. Its full name is The State of Rhode Island and Providence Plantations. Rhode Island is a New England state bordered on the west by Connecticut and on the north and east by Massachusetts. The Atlantic Ocean is to the south.

One story about Rhode Island's name begins in the Mediterranean Sea. The Greek island of Rhodes lies near the coast of Turkey. In 1524, an Italian sea captain, Giovanni da Verrazano, was exploring the eastern coast of North America. He came to Block Island, which is off the mainland of present-day Rhode Island. This island, he reported, is "about the bigness of the Island of the Rhodes." Block Island is actually much smaller than Rhodes.

The English colonists who came later thought that Verrazano was describing another island. They thought it was the large island that the Native Americans called Aquidneck, which lies at the mouth of Narragansett Bay. The colonists renamed the island Rhode Island.

Settlements on the mainland were called the Providence Plantations. Eventually, the mainland and island settlements were made one colony, which was named Rhode Island and Providence Plantations. When the colony became a state in 1776, it kept its long name. But people have always used the short form.

The Land and Climate
Rhode Island is only about 50 miles (80 km) long at its greatest length. Its greatest width is less than 50 miles (80 km). Of its total area, 165 square miles (427 sq. km) are water. The land area is 1,214 square miles (3,144 sq. km). With a population of just over 1 million, Rhode Island has more people per square mile than any other state, except New Jersey.

Rhode Island has 36 islands, most of which lie in the Narragansett Bay. Two of the bay's arms are called the Providence River and the Sakonnet River. Ten miles (16 km) out to sea is Block Island, named for Adriaen Block, a Dutch navigator. Its Great Salt Pond was turned into a harbor in 1900. A channel was dug to connect it to the ocean. The many bays and inlets of Rhode Island give it more than 380 miles (608 km) of shoreline, which is why it is known as "the Ocean State."

The rivers of the state are rather small, but they are useful. Their falls provide waterpower. The largest lake in the state is Scituate Reservoir, which was created by a dam across the Pawtuxet River. The lake supplies water to the city of Providence. Much of Rhode Island is made up of low, rounded hills.

On the whole, Rhode Island has a

RHODE ISLAND

Capital and largest city
Providence
(160,728 people)

Area
1,214 square miles
(3,114 sq. km)
Rank: 50th

Population
1,003,464 people
Rank: 42nd

Statehood
May 29, 1790
(Last of the original
13 states to ratify the
Constitution)

Principal rivers
Blackstone River
Pawtuxet River

Highest point
Jerimoth Hill,
812 feet (247 m),
near the Connecticut
border

Motto
"Hope"

Song
"Rhode Island"

Famous people
Ambrose Burnside,
George M. Cohan,
Nathanael Greene,
Christopher and Oliver
La Farge, Matthew C.
and Oliver Perry,
Gilbert Stuart

ATLANTIC OCEAN

Block I.
Block Island

STATE SYMBOLS

▲ **The early blue violet blooms between April and May.**

◀ **The state seal shows the state motto—"Hope"— above an anchor.**

▶ **The Rhode Island Red hen was bred more than 100 years ago in Rhode Island.**

▲ **The Red Maple, Rhode Island's state tree, is one of the loveliest of woodland trees.**

In Newport, Rhode Island, tourists can visit the oldest Quaker meetinghouse in America, the Friends Meeting House, built in 1699, and the oldest synagogue, the Touro Synagogue, built in 1763.

milder climate than the more northern areas of New England. Rhode Island's precipitation is about right for farming. However, hurricanes have caused flooding and other damage in low-lying areas.

History

When the first Europeans came to settle this region, five Native American tribes already lived there. The most important were the Narragansett and Wampanoag.

Rhode Island was settled chiefly by English colonists from Massachusetts. The Puritans in Massachusetts were hard on people who disagreed with them in matters of religion. In 1635, they told one such person, Roger Williams, to leave their colony. He bought land from the Narragansett Native Americans in what is now the state of Rhode Island. Williams named his settlement Providence; God's providence, or guidance, he said, had brought him there in his distress. The settlement is now the county and city of Providence, the state's capital.

Other people driven out of Massachusetts for the same reasons followed Roger Williams's example. They founded the towns of Portsmouth and Newport in 1638 and 1639. A fourth settlement, Warwick, was started south of Providence.

▲ A view of Providence, the capital and largest city in Rhode Island.

By 1654, all of these settlements became one colony. A paper signed by King Charles II in 1663 stated, among other things, that people in that colony were allowed to worship as they pleased.

Like the rest of New England, the colony suffered from war. Rhode Islanders fought the French more than once. They fought Native Americans, too. The Indian war of 1675–1676 started when settlers moved onto land held by the Wampanoag tribe. The powerful Narragansett soon joined the Wampanoags in their fight. Towns in Massachusetts and Rhode Island were destroyed.

Rhode Islanders needed money to buy manufactured goods from Britain. They earned it by trade—buying and selling. Rhode Island, like Massachusetts, took part in a three-cornered trade. Rum made in Rhode Island was carried to Africa and exchanged for slaves. The slaves were

▼ Newport Bridge connects the fashionable sailing and jazz-festival city of Newport, with the Rhode Island mainland.

◀ The Breakers was designed for the industrialist Cornelius Vanderbilt and his family. It is one of many grand mansions in Newport, Rhode Island, built during the late 1800s and early 1900s as summer houses for America's richest families.

taken to the sugar islands of the West Indies, where they were sold for molasses made from sugar. The molasses was brought back to Rhode Island for making rum. Every step in this trade earned a profit.

Newport was an important naval base during the Revolutionary War. Nathanael Greene, who was born in Rhode Island, was a leading American general in the revolution.

Industrial growth began in Rhode Island in the late 1700s. In 1790, an English industrialist, Samuel Slater, built the first successful spinning mill in the United States on the Blackstone River in present-day Pawtucket. (The restored mill still stands.) This mill spun cotton into yarn for weaving cloth. Other factories soon followed. People came to Rhode Island from Ireland, Italy, and eastern Europe to work in the factories. French Canadians also came.

Rhode Islanders at Work

In the 1900s, southern textile mills took much business away from New England, but some textiles are still manufactured in Rhode Island, along with jewelry, silverware, metal products, electronics equipment, and machine tools. Manufacturing is the state's main business. Most of the factories and their warehouse outlets are grouped in the region around Providence. The area stretches from Pawtucket in the north to Warwick in the south. Providence, the state's capital, is the second largest city in New England.

Most Rhode Islanders live in towns and cities. But this little state, in spite of its large population, has room for farms. Dairy herds supply milk to cities. Some farmers keep poultry. Chickens called *Rhode Island Reds* are a favorite breed. The crop that earns the most profit for farmers is potatoes. Apples, peaches, oats, and hay are also important crops. Perch, haddock, and other fish are caught in Rhode Island waters.

The first center of learning founded in Rhode Island was Rhode Island College, started in 1764. It is now Brown University.

Every summer, tourists come to Rhode Island to sail or go deep-sea fishing in the coastal waters. Yachts from other countries have met the best yachts from the United States in the America's Cup races off Newport. Visitors can see the impressive Newport houses built by U.S. industrial magnates of the 1900s. A mysterious round tower known as the Old Stone Mill in Newport was

▲ The Caspian tern is a fast-flying seabird found around the shores of Rhode Island.

▲ The herring gull is common along the eastern seaboard, including the waters around Rhode Island.

probably built by early colonists as part of a grain mill. But Henry Wadsworth Longfellow was one of the people who thought that Vikings had built it. The tower is mentioned in his poem "The Skeleton in Armor." The U.S. Navy has a large base in Newport.

▶▶▶▶ **FIND OUT MORE** ◀◀◀◀
Manufacturing; Massachusetts; Verrazano, Giovanni da; Vikings; Williams, Roger

▼ The influence of Cecil Rhodes was felt all across Africa. This contemporary cartoon shows him bestriding the continent like a colossus.

RHODES, CECIL (1853–1902)

Cecil John Rhodes was a British administrator and businessman in South Africa. He helped to extend British control over that region.

Rhodes was born in Hertfordshire, England, and was educated at Oxford University. He spent his college vacations working at the diamond mines in Kimberly, South Africa. He later gained control over all the South African diamond mines and founded the DeBeers Consolidated Mines Company.

Rhodes's greatest ambition was to increase the power of the British Empire. He persuaded the British to take over Bechuanaland (now Botswana). The British South Africa Company, which Rhodes had founded, opened new mines in the present-day regions of Zambia and Zimbabwe (known as Rhodesia—in honor of Rhodes—until 1979). These regions later became part of the British Empire.

Rhodes served as prime minister of the Cape Colony in South Africa from 1890 to 1896. He was forced to resign after a disastrous attempt to take over the Transvaal, an area already colonized by the Dutch.

Rhodes left a large sum of money in his will to be used as scholarships to Oxford University. The Rhodes Scholarships are awarded each year to students from several nations, including the United States.

▶▶▶▶ **FIND OUT MORE** ◀◀◀◀
Boer War; Diamond; South Africa; Zimbabwe

RHYME

SEE POETRY

RHYTHM

SEE DANCE, MUSIC, AND POETRY

RICE

Rice is one of the most important of all foods. It is the main food of millions of Asians. Rice is also eaten by other people in almost every country in the world.

Rice is a member of the family of cereal grasses, such as wheat, oats, and rye. There are many kinds of rice, but the kind most important for food has the name of *Oryza sativa*. It was developed from Asian wild rice.

People in Asia first sow rice seed in muddy, flooded fields. When the seedlings are a month to six weeks old, they are dug up and transplanted in even rows in *paddies*. Paddies are plowed fields covered with 3 or 4 inches (8 to 10 cm) of fresh water. The plants are pushed into the mud under the water and continue to grow in the paddies until they are harvested. The flooded fields are drained before the harvest.

Planting and harvesting of rice is done by hand in the Orient because many farmers there cannot afford to buy farm machinery. In other rice-growing areas, such as California, rice is planted by scattering seed from an airplane over a flooded field. The rice crop is harvested by machinery.

When ready for harvesting, the white rice grains have a coating of bran and are covered by a brown husk. The brown husk contains vitamins and minerals, but millions of people prefer the white grain, with the husks removed. This is called polished rice. In Asia, people who eat white rice, and almost nothing else, often suffer from *beriberi*. Beriberi is a disease that makes people unable to move their arms and legs. It comes from a shortage of the B-complex vitamins that are found in unpolished rice. Modern science has taught people that it is better to eat brown rice instead of white rice, because the brown rice contains the necessary B vitamins. As a result, the use of brown rice is increasing.

More than 90 percent of the world's rice is produced in Asiatic countries. Other main rice-growing countries are the United States, Spain, Brazil, Egypt, and Italy.

▶ ▶ ▶ ▶ **FIND OUT MORE** ◀ ◀ ◀ ◀
Agriculture; Asia; Buffalo;
Farm Machinery; Food; Grain;
Nutrition; Vitamins and Minerals

RICHARD, KINGS OF ENGLAND

Richard is the name of three kings of England.

Richard I (1157–1199) was the son of Henry II of England and Eleanor of Aquitaine. Richard became king when his father died in 1189. Richard I neglected his country and spent much of his reign fighting wars abroad. He was given the nickname the "Lion-Heart," because of his bravery in battle.

As soon as Richard was crowned king, he gathered an army and went on a *crusade* (holy war) to the Holy Land to free Jerusalem from the Muslims. The French king Philip Augustus also gathered an army and joined the crusade. The crusade ended in a truce, but Philip had

▲ Rice is a cereal grass that grows in warm, wet places. Rice seedlings need a lot of water, so they are grown in flooded fields, called *paddies*.

There are three types of rice used for cooking: short-, medium, and long-grain. Most of the world's rice is still harvested by hand. More than 300 million tons of rice is produced each year throughout the world.

▲ Richard I of England died of an arrow wound in battle. He had been fighting his former ally, **Philip Augustus of France.**

▼ The Peasants' Revolt took place during the reign of Richard II. The young king pacified the peasants when their leader was killed.

begun to plot against Richard.

On the return journey, Richard was captured by the Duke of Austria, a friend of Philip Augustus. Richard was held prisoner for three years until he was ransomed. When Richard finally returned to England, he started a war against Philip Augustus and was killed in battle.

Richard II (1367–1400) became king when he was only 10 years old. The kingdom was ruled by Richard's uncle, John of Gaunt, until the king grew up. Because Richard was so young, the nobles of England thought they had a chance to gain more power for themselves. They began to fight among themselves and against the king. When Richard grew up, he managed to win control of his kingdom. He put to death many of the rebellious nobles. But his enemies finally forced him to give up his throne. Richard's cousin, Henry of Lancaster, was then crowned King Henry IV.

Richard III (1452–1485) is said to have gained his throne by murder and treachery. Richard was the brother of King Edward IV. Edward had two young sons. When King Edward died in 1483, his elder son, who was 12 years old, was crowned King Edward V. Richard was named Edward's protector.

Richard had himself declared king. Richard's enemies, led by Henry Tudor, revolted against him. Richard was killed at the Battle of Bosworth

▲ Richard III was renowned for his generalship and his abilities as an administrator. He was a competent king, but made many enemies.

Field. Henry Tudor was then crowned King Henry VII. This was the end of the Wars of the Roses. Richard was accused of murdering his two young nephews. Richard's guilt is questioned by many historians. There is no proof that Richard murdered the young princes.

▶▶▶▶ **FIND OUT MORE** ◀◀◀◀

Crusades; Edward, Kings of England; Eleanor of Aquitaine; English History; Henry, Kings of England; John, King of England; Wars of the Roses

RIDING

SEE HORSEBACK RIDING

RIDDLE

A *riddle* is a puzzling question that requires some clever thinking to answer correctly. It may be a problem with a hidden solution to be discovered or guessed. Riddles have been popular since ancient times.

Early people took their riddles seriously, and often felt humiliated if they couldn't solve them. According to legend, the Greek poet Homer is said to have died of shame because he couldn't find the answer to a riddle. Prophets, oracles, and poets presented many riddles for ordinary people to solve.

In Greek mythology, a famous riddle was asked by the *Sphinx,* a winged monster with a lion's body and a woman's head. "What walks on four legs in the morning, two at noon, and three at night?" The Sphinx destroyed all those who were unable to give the correct answer. Oedipus solved the riddle: A person crawls on all fours when a baby, walks on two legs as an adult, and walks with a cane in old age. The Sphinx became so upset that she killed herself.

Riddles were very common in Europe during the Middle Ages. Here is an old English riddle: "When is a door not a door?" The answer, "When it is ajar." This kind of riddle is also called a *pun.* A pun is a play on words, using a word or words to suggest different meanings. A riddle whose answer is a pun is called a *conundrum.* Most modern riddles are conundrums. Two well-known riddles or conundrums are: "What has four wheels and flies?" A garbage truck. "What is black and white and read all over?" A newspaper.

A riddle with pictures is called a *rebus.* The pictures represent words, syllables, or sounds. A rebus may contain numbers, symbols, and letters, as well as drawings and words. One of the most familiar rebuses is the debtor's IOU for "I owe you."

▶▶▶▶ **FIND OUT MORE** ◀◀◀◀

Sphinx; Word Games

RIFLE

SEE GUNS AND RIFLES

RILEY, JAMES WHITCOMB (1849–1916)

James Whitcomb Riley was an American poet. He became known for his poetry written in the Indiana country *dialect* (regional type of speech). He wrote many poems for and about children. "Little Orphant Annie" is one of Riley's best-known poems. Little Orphant Annie was a young servant who told ghost stories at night. Each story ended with the frightening statement,

"An' the Gobble-uns'll git you
Ef you don't watch out!"

Riley, born in Greenfield, Indiana, is often called the "Hoosier Poet." (People who live in Indiana are called Hoosiers.) Riley left school at 16 and became a traveling sign painter. Later, he went to work for newspa-

Richard I reigned for ten years, but spent only six months of that time in England. After Richard II left the throne, he was held prisoner in Pontefract Castle. He died there, and it is thought that he was murdered. Richard III is said to have been a hunchback, but there is no evidence of this in his portraits.

▲ James Whitcomb Riley, the "Hoosier Poet."

pers in Greenfield and Indianapolis. Riley wrote poems for the *Indianapolis Journal,* and they soon became very popular. In 1883, his first book of poetry, *The Old Swimmin' Hole and 'Leven More Poems,* was published. Other books of Riley's poems include *Afterwhiles, Rhymes of Childhood, Poems Here at Home,* and *The Book of Joyous Children.* Riley's work shows an understanding of and fondness for the people of Indiana.

▶▶▶▶ **FIND OUT MORE** ◀◀◀◀
Indiana; Poetry

RIMSKY-KORSAKOV, NICOLAI (1844–1908)

▲ **Nicolai Rimsky-Korsakov, the Russian composer, began his career as an officer in the Russian navy.**

One of the most important musical figures in the 1800s was the Russian composer Nicolai Rimsky-Korsakov. He is probably best remembered for his romantic orchestral work, *Scheherezade.* Among Rimsky-Korsakov's famous pieces are "The Flight of the Bumble Bee," from the opera *Tsar Saltan,* and "Song of India," from the opera *Sadko.*

Rimsky-Korsakov was born in Tikhvin in northwestern Russia. At an early age, he displayed extraordinary musical talent. His parents, however, sent him to the naval academy at St. Petersburg. During a three-year naval cruise, Rimsky-Korsakov wrote his first symphony. In 1871, he left the navy and began composing music. He became part of "The Russian Five," consisting of Mili Balakirev, César Cui, Modest Moussorgsky, Aleksandr Borodin, and himself. This group wrote music in a distinctively Russian style. Rimsky-Korsakov's music contains many Russian folk themes.

Rimsky-Korsakov was a professor of musical composition at the St. Petersburg Conservatory for more than 35 years. He composed choral works, piano pieces, and overtures, as well as symphonies and operas. Several of his students, including Sergei Prokofiev and Igor Stravinsky, later became famous as composers and conductors.

▶▶▶▶ **FIND OUT MORE** ◀◀◀◀
Music; Opera; Orchestras and Bands; Prokofiev, Sergei; Stravinsky, Igor

RIO DE JANEIRO

Rio de Janeiro is the greatest port in Brazil and for a long time was the capital of that country. Few cities have so beautiful a setting as Rio de Janeiro. Its huge bay is lined with fine sand beaches such as the Copacabana. Mountain peaks form a backdrop. One peak, called Sugar Loaf, 1,325 feet (404 m) high, dominates the entrance to the bay. Another peak, *Corcovado* ("the Hunchback"), reaches 2,300 feet (700 m) and is crowned by a giant statue of Christ the Redeemer.

The people of Rio, often called *Cariocans,* come from every country in the world. Only one person in eight is of pure Portuguese descent. A cheerful and lively people, their love of life is best shown in the Mardi Gras Carnival the city celebrates every year before Lent. Cariocans love sport, and the largest football (soccer) stadium in the world is in Rio.

Rio is a busy marketing city for such important Brazilian products as coffee, cotton, and diamonds. The city has factories for clothing, food, metals, and chemicals. Rio's population is about 11 million people, which now ranks it the second largest city in Brazil in population, next to São Paulo.

Portuguese explorers visited the area about 1502. The French established a colony there in 1555, but they were soon driven out by the Portuguese. The traditional date of Rio's founding by the Portuguese is 1565. In the 1800s, when Brazil was a Por-

▲ **A giant statue of Christ stands above Rio de Janeiro.**

tuguese colony, the French general Napoléon occupied Portugal. The Portuguese royal family fled from Lisbon in Portugal to Rio de Janeiro and soon turned it into a splendid city. Rio de Janeiro was made the capital of independent Brazil in 1822 and remained so until 1960, when Brasilia became the capital.

▶▶▶▶ **FIND OUT MORE** ◀◀◀◀
Brazil; São Paulo

RIO GRANDE

The Rio Grande is the fifth longest river in North America. It forms the border between the United States and Mexico for almost 1,300 miles (2,100 km). The river flows a distance of more than 1,800 miles (2,900 km) from its source in the San Juan Mountains of southwestern Colorado. The Rio Grande grows wider as it flows through New Mexico. It meets Mexico at El Paso, Texas, and then flows southeastward forming the boundary. The Rio Grande often floods when rain comes in sudden cloudbursts. It emp-

ties into the Gulf of Mexico near Brownsville, Texas, and Matamoros, Mexico. (See the map with the article on the UNITED STATES OF AMERICA.)

Americans call this river the Rio Grande, which means "big river" in Spanish. Mexicans call it Rio Bravo, "mighty river." Cars and people can easily cross the river on several toll bridges between the United States and Mexico. An agreement between the two countries forbids all navigation on the river.

Farmers of both nations use Rio Grande water to irrigate their fields. Large dams, such as the Amistad Dam and Falcon Dam, have been constructed jointly by the United States and Mexico. The dams control floods and provide water for irrigation. Cotton, vegetables, and citrus fruits bloom in the lower Rio Grande Valley because of the irrigation water.

▶▶▶▶ **FIND OUT MORE** ◀◀◀◀
Mexican War; Mexico; River; Texas

RIVER

Most rivers begin life as streams of water in the mountains. The small streams flow downhill and join other streams to form a river that goes on to the sea or a lake. Melting snow and rain make the river larger. A stream that flows into a larger stream is called a *tributary*.

Did you know a river can be called young or old? A young river gathers water into a swift-running current. The water leaps down waterfalls and rapids on its way. The current breaks particles of soil and rock from the banks and carries them downstream. The particles "sandpaper" the sides and bed, or bottom, of the river and cut it deeper. This cutting action is called *erosion*. Such erosion may cut a canyon or gorge. The Grand Canyon of the Colorado River is the largest river canyon in the world.

▼ **In Big Bend National Park, the Rio Grande flows through this high, rocky canyon.**

▼ **The Yellowstone River plunges over a series of spectacular waterfalls into the breathtaking Grand Canyon of the Yellowstone.**

Melt-water — Glacier — Waterfall — Rapids — Stream — Tributary stream — River — Estuary — Spring — Flood plain — Oxbow lake — Meander — River mouth

By the time the river reaches "middle age," it has worn its valley down to a more gradual slope. The river has widened. The current moves more slowly. There is less erosion. The river forms broad loops, called *meanders*.

When the river reaches "old age," its current moves even more slowly. Particles of rock are deposited on the

▲ Most rivers start their lives in the mountains, fed by the rain and snow that fall there. Some begin as springs or as the melt-water from glaciers. At first, they flow quickly downhill, creating rapids and waterfalls and cutting deep gorges. Then, as the river moves onto lower ground, it flows more slowly. It becomes wider, is fed by tributary streams, and may form wide curves. As it reaches the sea, it sometimes breaks up into a number of channels.

▶ A meandering river changes its shape. Currents erode the outside curve, and mud and sand are deposited on the inside curve in the river. Eventually the wide loops that form are cut off to form oxbow lakes.

Meander — Loop widens — Oxbow lake

riverbed (making it shallower) and over the river's wide valley floor *(floodplain)* during times of flooding. The river meanders across the floodplain until it reaches the sea. Most rivers become very wide at their mouths, and some form deltas out of deposited sediment.

The people who first inhabited North America, like people everywhere, usually settled along rivers. The river provided drinking, cooking, and washing water. The people could catch fish. The river provided a natural highway—all you had to do was build a boat or barge. When people began to raise crops, river valleys provided fertile soil.

THE LONGEST RIVERS IN THE WORLD		
River	Approximate length (miles/kilometers)	Location
Nile	4,160/6,695	Africa
Amazon	3,900/6,276	South America
Mississippi-Missouri System	3,860/6,212	North America
Chang Jiang (Yangtze)	3,600/5,793	Asia
Ob-Irtysh System	3,010/4,844	Asia
Yellow (Hwang Ho)	3,010/4,844	Asia
Congo	2,900/4,667	Africa
Parana	2,700/4,345	South America
Lena	2,650/4,265	Asia
Mackenzie River	2,635/4,241	North America
Niger	2,600/4,184	Africa
Yenisei	2,570/4,136	Asia
Mekong	2,500/4,023	Asia
Mississippi	2,350/3,782	North America
Missouri	2,315/3,726	North America
Murray-Darling System	2,310/3,717	Australia

Today, farmers still cultivate river valleys. But people have learned to use river water before it drains into the sea. Huge dams, which interrupt the flow of the water, can turn turbines and generate electricity. Reservoirs collect river water and pipe it to cities and parched fields. Rivers that once carried Native American canoes now carry huge ships.

▶▶▶▶ **FIND OUT MORE** ◀◀◀◀

Dam; Flood; Irrigation; Waterfall; Water Supply

ROADS

SEE STREETS AND ROADS

ROBIN HOOD

According to legend, the outlaw and hero Robin Hood came from a noble family and lived in England during the 1100s. When he was a boy, he killed a man accidentally and was forced to flee into Sherwood Forest. He dressed in dark green clothing and became highly skilled with a bow and arrow. Robin Hood lived in the forest, where he befriended and gathered a loyal band of "merry men," including Friar Tuck, Little John, Will Scarlet, and Alan-a-Dale. Maid Marian, Robin Hood's lady love, shared in many of his adventures.

Robin first met Little John one day on a bridge. Neither would let the other pass. Little John, who was 7 feet (2 m) tall and very strong, toppled Robin Hood into the stream. Robin immediately asked Little John to join his men.

Robin delighted in robbing the rich and giving their money to the poor. The Sheriff of Nottingham tried unsuccessfully again and again to capture Robin. Robin died when a treacherous cousin, pretending to help him, actually caused him to bleed to death. Some people think that Robin Hood was the Earl of Huntingdon, a Saxon who lost his lands to the invading Normans.

ROBINSON, JACKIE (1919–1972)

Jackie Robinson was the first black player in American major-league baseball. He was an outstanding athlete in every sport that he played.

Jack Roosevelt Robinson was born on a poor sharecropper's farm in Cairo, Georgia. His family moved to Pasadena, California, where he grew up. In high school, Jackie worked at part-time jobs, but he also managed to play on his school's football, basketball, baseball, and track teams. He starred in football, baseball, and track at the University of California at Los Angeles. He was also the National Collegiate broad jumping champion in 1940.

Robinson became a lieutenant in the U.S. Army during World War II. After the war, he played with black leagues, because no blacks were allowed in Major League baseball. Brooklyn Dodgers' general manager Branch Rickey was determined to integrate baseball and signed Robinson to play. Robinson's career with the Dodgers lasted from 1947 until 1956. During that time, the Dodgers won six National League pennants and one World Series.

In 1962, he became the first black player elected to the Baseball Hall of Fame. But he will be remembered most for the character and strength he demonstrated in breaking baseball's color barrier.

▶▶▶▶ **FIND OUT MORE** ◀◀◀◀
Baseball

▲ The legendary English outlaw and hero Robin Hood is said to have been a skilled archer. His weapon was the longbow, made of yew wood. His arrows were tipped with goose feathers.

▲ Jackie Robinson leaps nimbly over a player sliding into second base.

▲ In films and stories, robots often resemble human beings, but in real life this is rarely true. This robot, called Robby, appeared in the film *Forbidden Planet*.

▼ Industrial robots can do many different jobs. This is Unimate, made by the firm Unimation. As well as moving objects from place to place, it can also weld metal.

⚙ ROBOT

A *robot* is a machine that can perform acts or work a person does. The word *robot* comes from the Czech word for work—*robots*—and was first used in a play about robots written by the Czech writer Karel Capek in the 1920s. At that time, a robot was only an idea, but recently simple robots have become a reality.

If a robot is going to act like a person, it cannot simply *act*—it must also *react*. It must be able to change what it is doing as the situation changes. If you are riding your bicycle toward an intersection and you see a car coming, you know to stop. You react to the car by changing what you are doing. The bicycle does not react. If it weren't for you, it would roll into the intersection and cause an accident.

In order to react, the robot must be able to pick up information from outside itself and compare this infor-mation with what it already knows and what it wants to do. From this comparison, it must decide what to do next. All of this must be done in an instant.

Robots should not be confused with sophisticated remote control devices. These perform tasks such as handling radioactive materials or working with bomb disposal teams. But they are not really robots at all, because they do not carry out their tasks automatically. They are opera-tor-controlled, a useful extension of their human masters.

The electronic computer has made it possible for a robot

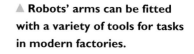

▲ Robots' arms can be fitted with a variety of tools for tasks in modern factories.

to sort out information and react quickly. The perfect robot—one that could do everything a person can do—has not yet been made. Most robots can do certain limited things and react to certain kinds of changes. An automatic pilot in an airplane "reads" the airplane's instruments and steers the plane the way a human pilot would. But it can-not get out of the plane and drive a car home. Robotlike machines can be programmed to do jobs in a factory. They work at welding, paint spray-ing, loading and unloading, or feed-ing parts into machines. Certain robots can be used as substitutes for human beings in scientific research. Few of these robots look like people. One robot that does look like a per-son was built to test space suits for the astronauts. This robot can bend like a human being can, shrug its shoulders, and even dance. A robot has been built that keeps itself safe. This robot knows not to walk downstairs, because it might fall. Whenever its batteries get low, the robot carefully plugs itself into an electrical outlet and systematically recharges its own power packs.

▶▶▶▶ **FIND OUT MORE** ◀◀◀◀
Computer

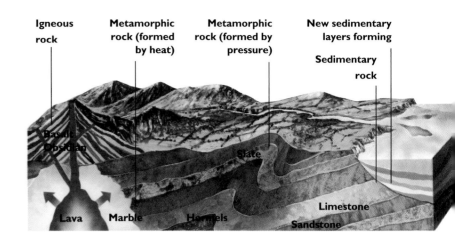

Igneous rock | Metamorphic rock (formed by heat) | Metamorphic rock (formed by pressure) | New sedimentary layers forming

Sedimentary rock

Basalt
Obsidian

Slate

Lava   Marble   Hornfels

Limestone
Sandstone

 ## ROCK

The whole Earth is covered by a crust of rock from 15 to 40 miles (24 to 64 km) thick. Most of this crust is covered by water and soil, but in many places the rocky crust is bare.

Rock is a solid material made up of minerals. The minerals vary and are not always combined in the same proportions. The rock called granite contains several minerals. The mineral called orthoclase may make up one quarter to one-half of the granite. The mineral quartz may make up one-tenth to one-quarter. And the other minerals vary between one-fifth and one-quarter each. Pieces of granite with different proportions of each mineral may have different weights, colors, and textures.

Kinds of Rock
There are three main kinds of rocks on earth: *igneous, sedimentary*, and *metamorphic.*

IGNEOUS ROCKS. Igneous, or firemade, rocks come from molten rock, called *magma*, which lies under the Earth's crust. From time to time, masses of magma push slowly upward through the crust. The rising magma cools and hardens. Millions of years later, the crust above the cooled magma may be worn away by *erosion*. Then, the mass of igneous rock is exposed to view.

Sometimes, the rising magma reaches cracks or weak places in the

▲ Syenite is a form of granite, which is an igneous rock.

crust. It flows out upon the surface of the Earth through volcanoes or through long cracks, called *fissures*. Magma that reaches the Earth's surface is called *lava*. Parts of Oregon, Washington, and Idaho were formed by immense flows of lava from the volcanoes. Granite and basalt are the two most common igneous rocks.

SEDIMENTARY ROCKS. The rocks on the Earth's surface are continually being broken up into small grains through the action of weather, running water, wind, glaciers, and gravity. Running water carries away most of the rock grains, called *sediment*. Mud, clay, and sand are kinds of sediment. The sediment piles up at the mouths of rivers or wherever the water slows down enough so that it can sink to the bottom.

When sediment is piled to great depths, the weight of the upper layers

▲ The different layers of rock that make up the Earth's crust are known as *strata*. There are three main types of rock (igneous, sedimentary, and metamorphic), all of which are formed in different ways.

▲ Granite and basalt are both formed from volcanic lava, which has cooled at different rates.

▲ Sandstone is a sedimentary rock. As its name suggests, it is made up of grains of sand.

Chalk

Limestone

▲ **Limestone and chalk are formed from the skeletons of millions of tiny sea creatures.**

WHERE TO DISCOVER MORE

Gallant, Roy A. *Our Restless Earth*. New York: Watts, 1986.

Symes, R.F. *Rocks and Minerals*. New York: Knopf, 1988.

presses down on the lower layers with tremendous force. This squeezes water out from between the grains. Sometimes the water contains dissolved minerals that act as cement. Eventually, all the water is squeezed out, and the grains are pressed together into a solid mass of rock—this is called sedimentary rock.

Rock fragments are not the only source of sedimentary rock. Large areas of the Earth are covered with a rock called limestone. Coral animals, shellfish, and the tiny plants called *diatoms* take a mineral called *calcium carbonate* out of seawater. They use it to form their skeletons or shells. When they die, they sink to the bottom of the sea. In millions of years, their broken skeletons and shells pile up in layers thousands of feet thick. Pressure eventually changes these layers into limestone. Chalk is a kind of limestone. Limestone is also formed from calcium carbonate deposited by water.

METAMORPHIC ROCKS. When masses of magma push upward into the Earth's crust, sedimentary or igneous rocks nearby are heated and put under pressure. The heat and pressure may change these rocks to metamorphic, or "changed-form," rock. For example, limestone is changed to marble, and the rock called shale is changed to slate. Rock may also be *metamorphosed*, (changed into a different form) because of shifts in the Earth's crust.

Slate

Marble

▲ **Slate and marble are metamorphic rocks, formed by heat and pressure.**

2280

▶▶▶▶ **FIND OUT MORE** ◀◀◀◀
Earth; Erosion; Geology; Granite; Mineral; Volcano

ROCKEFELLER FAMILY

The Rockefeller family is noted for its activities in business, politics, and *philanthropy* (donating money to worthy causes). The wealth and fame of this family began with John D. Rockefeller (1839–1937), who came from a poor family in upstate New York. As a young man he made money by trading grain.

Rockefeller invested in oil and went on to build the Standard Oil Company. This company was so successful that he became the world's richest man before he was 40.

Many people questioned Rockefeller's business practices, but by the 1890s, he turned to philanthropy. He helped establish the University of Chicago in 1890, and went on to found many institutions to support academic research, medical improvements, and the arts. During his lifetime, he gave away $550 million.

▲ **A gold statue of Prometheus in a fountain outside the Rockefeller Center, in New York.**

His son, John D. Rockefeller Jr. (1874–1960), and grandson John D. Rockefeller III (1906–1978) continued the tradition of philanthropy.

Another grandson, Nelson A. Rockefeller (1908–1979), entered politics. He was governor of New York from 1959 to 1973 and Vice President of the United States under Gerald Ford, from 1974 to 1977.

John D. Rockefeller IV (1937–), the son of John D. Rockefeller III, is also in politics. He has served West Virginia as governor from 1977 to 1985 and as U.S. senator since 1985.

ROCKET

You can make a very simple rocket out of a balloon. Just fill the balloon with air and let it go. The air rushes out of the mouth of the balloon, and the balloon flies across the room.

The balloon is a compressed-air rocket. When you blow into it, you force a large amount of air into a small space. The rubber of the balloon stretches from the air pressure. The air pushes in all directions equally and, if the mouth of the balloon is closed, is contained by an equal force in all directions (See illustration A, upper right). But both the air and the rubber of the balloon are elastic, and if the mouth of the balloon is open, the air under pressure rushes out of it (illustration B). The rubber of the balloon begins to shrink to its normal size. The pressure of the air inside the balloon is now much greater in the direction opposite the mouth than that at the mouth. The balloon flies in the direction opposite the mouth. All rockets work on this principle. By allowing a gas under pressure to escape from the end, they are driven in the direction opposite to that end.

Compressed air is a kind of pro-pellant, but it is not a powerful pro-pellant. As in fireworks, rockets use a propellant that burns, giving off a hot gas that pushes the rocket at high speeds through the air.

The gas does not have to push against anything. This is one reason why a rocket can move through empty space. Another reason is that the rocket propellant carries its own oxygen. Burning is just a rapid kind of *oxidation*—the combining of oxygen and another substance. All burning requires oxygen. A jet engine gets its oxygen from the air, so a jet can only fly in air. A rocket carries its own oxygen, so it can fly in empty space. A complete rocket propellant includes a *fuel* that burns and an *oxidizer* that makes the fuel burn. Some fuels and oxidizers will burn on contact. Others need a spark to set them off. Rockets can use solid or liquid propellants.

In a simple solid-propellant engine, the propellant is a solid cake, or *grain,* attached to the inner walls of a tubular casing. The grain contains both the oxidizer and the fuel. The casing serves as the container for the propellant and as the combustion chamber. An opening, which is often star-shaped, through the middle of the grain allows the grain to burn evenly outward. A nozzle at the open end of the casing controls the flow of hot gases.

A liquid-fuel engine has separate fuel and oxidizer. The propellants are held in tanks outside the combustion chamber and are fed into the chamber by pumps or by pressurized gas.

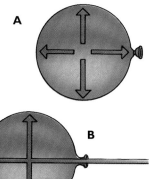

▲ A balloon can be made to act like a simple rocket. When the balloon mouth is opened, the air under pressure rushes out.

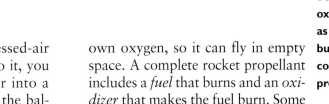

▲ A liquid fuel rocket. Separate tanks contain liquid oxygen and a propellant such as liquid hydrogen. The two burn together in the combustion chamber, producing very hot gases.

The first liquid fuel rocket was built by Dr. Robert Goddard in 1926. The fuel he used was petrol and the oxidizer, liquid oxygen. Here, the rocket stands on its launch frame. It flew for only two seconds after being launched.

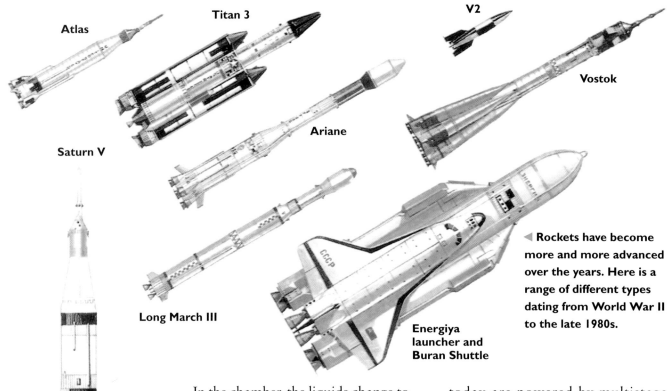

Atlas

Titan 3

V2

Vostok

Saturn V

Ariane

Long March III

Energiya
launcher and
Buran Shuttle

◀ Rockets have become
more and more advanced
over the years. Here is a
range of different types
dating from World War II
to the late 1980s.

▲ Saturn V is a multistage
rocket. By the time the
capsule is projected into
orbit, more than nine-tenths
of the rocket has been
discarded.

In the chamber, the liquids change to vapor and are ignited. The flow of hot gases produced is controlled by a nozzle.

The liquid-fuel engine has several advantages over the solid fuel engine. Its performance is usually higher, as measured by the velocity of the exhaust gases. The flow and burning of liquid fuel is easier to control, and a liquid-fuel engine can be turned off and on. Liquid-fuel engines are usually more powerful. The most powerful liquid-fuel rocket that has been publicized is the Russian Energya. It is more powerful than the Saturn V, whose first-stage engines produce 7,570,000 pounds (3,435,000 kg) of thrust. Saturn V was used for the Apollo and Skylab programs. The most powerful solid-fuel rocket engines are the two boosters used on the Space Shuttle.

The Chinese used rockets in warfare in the A.D. 1200s. For the next several hundred years, most rockets were designed as weapons. Then, in the late 1800s, a Russian scientist, Konstantin Tsiolkovsky, suggested that rockets could be used in space travel. He proposed the *multistage*, or *step*, rocket. Most space flights today are powered by multistage rockets.

The multistage rocket consists of several rocket engines set one on top of another. The booster, or first stage engine, is fired first. When the first stage has burned up its fuel, it drops away, and the second stage ignites. When the second stage has exhausted its fuel, the third stage ignites. Most multistage rockets have three stages. The multiple staging allows the rockets to use a powerful booster to provide the initial launching thrust without having to carry the weight of the booster throughout the flight.

Tsiolkovsky also proposed using liquid fuel for rockets. In 1926, Dr. Robert Goddard, an American scientist, built the first liquid-fuel rocket.

The 10-foot (3-m) long rocket flew 184 feet (56 m) in about 2½ seconds on its maiden flight. This flight marked the beginning of modern rocketry. Most large rockets since then have used liquid fuel.

During World War II, the most important advances in rocketry were made in Germany. German V-2 rockets with explosive warheads were fired across the English Channel, badly damaging the city of London

ROCKETS USED IN THE MANNED SPACE PROGRAM OF THE UNITED STATES

Rocket	Height (ft/m)	Stages	Thrust (lb/kg)	Diameter(ft/m)	Fuel	Importance
Redstone	83/25.3	I	82,000/37,200 a liquid fuel	5.7/1.7	Aerozine 50	Sent America's first man into space (Alan Shepard) aboard Mercury spacecraft
Atlas (Series D)	67/20.4	1½	360,000/163,300	10/3	Kerosene and liquid oxygen	First launch vehicle in the free world to orbit a man (John Glenn). Also, the first operational intercontinental ballistic missile (ICBM).
Titan II	103/31.4	2	530,000/240,400	10/3	Nitrogen tetroxide and mixture of hydrazine and dimethyl hydrazine	Launched the Gemini spacecraft
Saturn V	364/111	3	(1) 7,570,000/3,400,000	(1) 33/10	Kerosene and liquid oxygen	Launched Apollo spacecraft to the moon
			(2)1,000,000/453,600	(2) 33/10	Liquid hydrogen & liquid oxygen	
			(3) 200,000/90,700	(3) 21.7/6.6	Liquid oxygen & liquid hydrogen	

and killing many civilians.

Since the war, the most important research has been carried on in the United States and Russia. Both countries have built many rockets for space exploration and military use. In 1957, the first man-made satellite, the Soviet *Sputnik I,* was launched by rocket. Shortly afterward, the first U.S. satellite, *Explorer I,* was launched by a Redstone rocket.

The Apollo space flights were powered by Saturn rockets. These multistage liquid-fuel rockets were 364 feet (111 m) high and were powerful enough to carry more than 50 tons (45 metric tons) to the moon. These were not the only rockets used on the Apollo flights. Smaller rockets were fired to change the direction of flight and to soften the spacecrafts' landings on the moon.

The Space Shuttle employs a combination of two separate solid-fuel boosters and a liquid-fuel engine in the shuttle to reach orbit. Both the boosters and the shuttle itself are designed to be used again. Only the tank for the liquid fuels is discarded. The Space Shuttle made its first flight in 1981 and has continued to conduct scientific research flights well into the 1990s.

▶ ▶ ▶ ▶ **FIND OUT MORE** ◀ ◀ ◀ ◀
Goddard, Robert H.; Jet Propulsion; Physics; Space Research; Space Travel

◀ **The Chinese invented the first firework rocket, but they also fired rockets as weapons of war.**

QUIZ

1. What kind of propellant do rockets use?
2. Which type of propellant is better: solid or liquid?
3. Who built the first liquid-fuel rocket?
4. What was the first man-made satellite launched by rocket?
5. When did the Space Shuttle make its *maiden* (first) flight?

(Answers on page 2304)

ROCK MUSIC

SEE POPULAR MUSIC

ROCKY MOUNTAINS

The Rocky Mountains extend through the western part of North America from Alaska all the way to Mexico. The "Rockies" provide magnificent scenery for those who live in or visit Alaska, Washington, Montana, Idaho, Wyoming, Utah, Colorado, and New Mexico. Most of the highest mountain peaks in North America are in the Rockies. Within the Rockies are many individual mountain ranges. (See the map with the article on NORTH AMERICA.)

The Rocky Mountains were formed 65 to 100 million years ago as volcanic action pushed the Earth's crust upward thousands of feet. The Rockies are about 150 million years younger than the Appalachians, whose more rounded shapes show the effects of erosion over a longer period.

Pacific Ocean winds drop their moisture when they reach the cool, high mountains, and most rainfall and snowfall occurs on the western side of the Rocky Mountains. High plateaus called "parks" lie between the ranges. Vegetation is heavier in the parks. The higher peaks stay snow-covered all year round. Low stretches of hot, dry desert are found in the southern Rockies.

The highest peak in the Rockies is Mount Elbert, 14,431 feet (4,399 m) high, in Colorado. The Continental Divide runs along the highest peaks of the Rockies and cuts through North America from north to south. Rivers in the United States west of the Divide flow toward the Pacific Ocean, and many east of the Divide flow toward the Mississippi River.

Every year, many tourists visit Yellowstone National Park or the Grand Canyon, which the Colorado River has made by cutting through the Rockies. In Canada, Banff National Park and Jasper National Park, in the Canadian Rockies, present scenic snowcapped mountains and glaciers. Ski resorts are very popular here.

Goats and bighorn sheep live high in the Rockies. Bears, deer, coyotes, mountain lions, and other animals live in the forests lower down.

When the pioneers reached the Rockies from the Great Plains, they were faced with mountains that seemed impossible to cross. But caravans on horseback and in wagons moved along the Oregon Trail through mountain passes to the Northwest. Some of the passes were discovered during the Lewis and Clark Expedition of 1804 to 1806. Stagecoaches later traveled through the mountains. Trains later replaced the stagecoaches.

Among the first white people to settle in the Rockies were prospectors searching for minerals. Today, mining is an important industry in the Rocky Mountain states. Rich veins of copper, lead, silver, gold, and zinc run through the mountains. There are also valuable deposits of oil, of shale, natural gas, phosphate, and *bituminous* (soft) coal.

▶ ▶ ▶ ▶ **FIND OUT MORE** ◀ ◀ ◀ ◀
Continental Divide; Grand Canyon; Mountain; Yellowstone National Park

---

The area covered by the Rocky Mountain states is more than one-fourth of the entire United States.

▼ The Rocky Mountains contain some of North America's most spectacular scenery. The Teton range in Wyoming is one of the most beautiful areas.

ROCOCO ART

In the 1700s in Europe, a style of art and architecture known as *Rococo* became popular. It spread all across Europe, including England. Rococo was a decorated, sentimental style. Rococo decor drew its inspiration from natural objects in which the lines move freely—flowers, vines, seaweed, and above all, seashells.

Ceres (the Roman goddess of agriculture), by the French painter Jean Antoine Watteau, National Gallery of Art, Washington, D.C., Samuel H. Kress Collection.

The style had its beginnings in the churches and palaces of the south German provinces. The German princes wanted their territories to have beautiful churches and palaces of which they could be proud. The 1700s were a time of deep religious feeling. And Rococo in church architecture was graceful and enthusiastic of spirit. Church interiors were often white and gold. Two families, the Asams and the Zimmermanns, created the German *Baroque* style, which soon became indistinguishable from Rococo.

Perhaps the foremost decorator of this age was the Venetian painter Giovanni Battista Tiepolo. He created *frescoes* (paintings on damp plaster) on the ceilings of many churches and palaces of the 1700s. His fresco painting on this page is *Nobility and Virtue*. He painted it in the Rezzonico Palace in the city of Venice. See Nobility and Virtue flying on the wings of a huge bird, while cherubs dart happily through the clouds.

The age of Rococo, besides producing fancy decor, was a great age for the creation of music in the German and Austrian provinces. Johann Sebastian Bach, Domenico Scarlatti, and George Frederick Handel wrote Baroque and Rococo music, whose trills and embellishments seem to fit in with the architecture of the time. Such music was often played in the salon of the castle of Sans Souci in Potsdam, the home of King Freder-

ick the Great. A great patron of music, King Frederick was a musician himself and played the flute very well. He entertained the composer Bach there, too. The Rococo setting seems made for a small music group. The white walls are decorated with

gold flowers, cherubs, and the ever-present shell design in various interpretations. Even the music stand has the twisted, intricate lines of Rococo.

The great painter of the age of Rococo was Antoine Watteau. He was born in Belgium, settled in France, and died at the young age of 37. He caught the delicate shades of feeling of the age of Rococo. Like Tiepolo, he designed interior decorations for the castles of the nobility. His dreams and ideals and his preference for dainty colors and delicate decoration expressed the feeling of Rococo. See the beauty of line in his oval painting on this page of *Ceres*, the Roman goddess who protected grain and summer's growing season.

Nobility and Virtue, part of a ceiling fresco by the Italian painter Giovanni Battista Tiepolo.

▲ This salon in a house in Paris, France, was decorated in the 1730s. The style is elaborate but graceful.

▲ A *clavichord*—a musical instrument similar to a harpsichord—made in the 1720s. The decorated wood is typical of the Rococo style.

Ceres is carrying a scythe, as the goddess of grain. Watteau loved to draw and paint beautiful girls. His folds of drapery shimmer, and he is a master of detail. Watteau expresses the spirit of Rococo—a lovely goddess sitting on a cloud, happy and serene.

Rococo influenced every kind of art. Opera houses all over Europe and Latin America were Rococo in design. Even Rococo knife handles and teapots were popular at that time. It became an elegant, international style, dedicated to happiness.

▶ ▶ ▶ ▶ **FIND OUT MORE** ◀ ◀ ◀ ◀
Bach Family; Baroque Period; Handel, George Frederick; Haydn, Franz Joseph; Mozart, Wolfgang Amadeus

RODENT

There are more than 1,700 different kinds of rodents in the world. In other words, about one-third of all the types of mammals in the world are rodents. Some of the best-known members of the rodent family are squirrels, guinea pigs, rats, mice, beavers, porcupines, chipmunks, hamsters, gerbils, chinchillas, prairie dogs, and gophers.

Rodents are gnawing animals; all of these animals have very sharp front teeth. These front teeth are called *incisors*. The incisors of a rodent keep growing as long as the animal lives. The rodent is constantly gnawing on things. In this way it keeps wearing away the tops of its incisors. If the rodent did not do this, its incisors would grow so long that it could not close its mouth or eat anything. But if the incisors did not grow, they would become worn away, and the rodent would not be able to eat properly.

The gnawing done by rodents also keeps their incisors very, very sharp. Always be very careful when you are handling pet rodents, such as hamsters. Their sharp teeth can give you a

▲ Two young gerbils.

▲ Hamsters are very popular as children's pets.

very nasty bite. If you are bitten, immediately ask an adult to treat the wound with a medical disinfectant. Some rodents can even gnaw through wire and glass if necessary.

◀ The flying squirrel (left) glides through the air using flaps of skin between its forelegs and its hindlegs. The chipmunk (below) lives mainly on the ground.

Most rodents eat grain, seeds, and nuts, but some eat almost anything. Many rodents store away extra food for the winter. Rodents live almost everywhere throughout the world. They have many different habitats. Some live in lakes and streams, and others live in trees. Many rodents live on the ground, and some live underground, in burrows. When winter

comes, many rodents *hibernate* in their burrows. That is, they go to sleep until warmer weather comes. Some rodents, like the chipmunk, sleep all winter long. Others, like the squirrel and hamster, wake up now and then to eat a bit of food. Rodents range in size from tiny mice to the South American capybara, which is about as large as a pig. Most rodents, however, are only about the size of a rat. The smallest rodent of all is the northern pygmy mouse, found in Mexico and parts of Texas and Arizona. Including its tail, it is just over 4 inches (10 cm) long. Another very small rodent, the mole, eats its own weight in leaves, seeds, and roots every day!

▶ ▶ ▶ ▶ **FIND OUT MORE** ◀ ◀ ◀ ◀
Animal; Animal Distribution; Animal Homes; Animal Kingdom; Beaver; Groundhog; Ground Squirrel; Guinea Pigs, Hamsters and Gerbils; Lemming; Mammal; Porcupine; Prairie Dog; Rats and Mice; Squirrel

RODEO

The rodeo is an exciting spectator sport that is held in the United States, Canada, and Australia. It is a contest of skill in roping cattle and riding wild horses (called broncos or broncs) and wild bulls. Cowboys and cowgirls need strength, courage, and speed to work in a rodeo. The animals are strong and dangerous, and each event is timed.

Some professional cowboys and cowgirls travel from one rodeo to another and live on the money they earn from winning rodeo events. Most rodeo performers belong to the Rodeo Cowboys Association. They pay a fee to enter an event, but they can win a great deal of money.

Rodeo competition began in the southwestern United States about 100 years ago. The word *rodeo* comes from the Spanish word for

▲ The alpine marmot, a type of ground squirrel, lives in mountainous areas. While they feed, they post *sentinels* (guards) to warn of predators.

▲ Covered wagon racing is one of the many exciting events that take place at a rodeo show.

roundup. When the hard work of rounding up the cattle from the range was over, the cowhands invented racing and roping contests for fun. Soon the idea spread to towns all over the West. Before long, rodeos were a money-making business.

Cheyenne, Wyoming, has a famous rodeo each year called Frontier Days.

▲The most famous sport at the rodeo is bronco-busting. The cowboys may ride bareback or use saddles. They are allowed to hold on only with one hand.

Pendleton, Oregon, has its Roundup, and Calgary, Alberta, in Canada, has the Stampede.

Rodeo arenas have wooden passageways, called *chutes*, at one end. In the riding events, a cowboy or cowgirl climbs onto a half-wild horse or bull while it is still in the chute. The door of the chute is opened, and when the animal is released, it comes leaping out. The rider tries to stay on for a certain length of time.

Saddle bronco riding is one of the oldest events. A bucking, leaping horse called a bucking bronco must be ridden for usually ten seconds. The rider is allowed to hold on with only one hand and must spur the horse constantly. *Spurs* are pieces of metal worn on a rider's boot heel to dig into the horse so it will move faster. But riders are not allowed to hurt the horses. *Bareback bronco riding* is riding a bronco without a saddle. The rider must hold onto the belt around the horse's middle with only one hand. He or she must spur the horse constantly and stay on for eight

seconds. *Bull riding* is the most dangerous event. A wild bull can crush a fallen rider with its hoofs or gore him or her with its horns. The cowboy or cowgirl must ride the bull bareback, just as in the bareback bronco event, for eight seconds.

Calf roping shows off the partnership of a cowboy or cowgirl and a horse. The horse and rider race after a calf. One end of the rider's rope is tied to the saddle horn; the other is made into a noose. The rider throws the noose around the calf's neck and then jumps off the horse. The well trained horse stands still, holding the rope tight. The cowboy or cowgirl throws the calf down and ties up three of its legs. The winner of this event is the person who ropes and ties a calf in the least amount of time. *Bulldogging* is a kind of animal wrestling. The rider and horse first catch up with a running *steer* (an ox raised for its beef). The rider leaps from the horse, grabs the steer by its horns, and forces it to the ground. Here again, the winner is the cowboy or cowgirl who completes the event in less time than any of the other contestants.

Clowns are an important part of the rodeo, too. They are as funny as any circus clown, but they have the responsibility of protecting fallen riders. The clowns draw the attention of the wild bulls away from fallen riders. This allows time for the riders to get up or be rescued.

Children also compete in rodeos as amateurs. The events in these rodeos are not so dangerous. Rodeo associations for junior, high school, and college-age groups sponsor hundreds of rodeos each year.

▶▶▶▶ **FIND OUT MORE** ◀◀◀◀
Cattle; Cowboy; Horseback Riding

RODGERS, RICHARD

SEE MUSICAL COMEDY

RODIN, AUGUSTE
(1840–1917)

The French sculptor François Auguste René Rodin has often been called the "Father of Modern Sculpture." He also is considered the greatest romantic sculptor. Romantic art stressed emotions and the imagination over reason and self-discipline. Rodin's statues and carvings have become world famous.

Rodin was born in Paris, France, where he studied drawing and sculpture. The first exhibition of his sculpture, in 1864, was a failure. In 1875, he traveled to Italy, where he studied the sculptures of the great Renaissance artist Michelangelo. Upon returning to Paris, Rodin set to work creating a very strong, lifelike figure of a person, entitled *The Age of Bronze*. The figure was so real-looking that many people thought Rodin had cast it from a live person, instead of from a clay model. The French government bought the statue and gave Rodin a free studio in which to work.

In 1880, Rodin did a set of sculptures for the entrance of the Museum of Decorative Arts in Paris. *The Thinker* (shown here) was one of those statues. You can see the power and energy in *The Thinker's* body. Although he is sitting quietly, his body shows that there is something on his mind. His leg and arm muscles are tense. His feet are pointed inward, and his toes are curled. His head rests on his hand, while his whole body is bent over in intense concentration. His left hand looks relaxed, but you get the feeling that any minute he may spring into action. Rodin, like Michelangelo, sculpted the human body so that the viewer could sense the thoughts and emotions that were happening inside.

In *The Thinker*, you see a powerful, muscular person. But he is a modern person, who must use his mind rather than his muscles if he is to figure out the rapid changes taking place in the surrounding world.

In 1900, a great exhibition of Rodin's sculpture brought him worldwide fame. Ever since then, his sculpture has had an enormous influence on artists throughout the world. People felt in Rodin's art the struggles and problems of modern people.

Apart from *The Thinker*, Rodin's most famous sculpture is *The Kiss*, a bronze of a man and woman embracing.

▶ ▶ ▶ ▶ **FIND OUT MORE** ◀ ◀ ◀
Art; Art History;
Michelangelo Buonarroti; Sculpture

ROGERS, WILL (1879–1935)

William Penn Adair Rogers was a popular U.S. humorist. He was born in Oologah, Native American Territory, in what is now Oklahoma. He was part Cherokee. Rogers was a cowboy in Texas for several years and then traveled with a Wild West show. He became a vaudeville actor in 1905.

Rogers performed astonishing tricks on stage with his *lariat* (rope for catching animals). At the same time, he entertained the audience with short, funny comments. Rogers appeared in the musical revues called the *Ziegfeld Follies*, in motion pictures, and in plays. He wrote amusing articles for *The New York Times* and other newspapers and published several books. He also was the host of a radio program. He pretended to be a simple, homespun kind of person. But he really had a sharp, clever mind that saw through the foolishness of others.

Rogers was killed in a plane crash in Alaska during a flight with Wiley Post, a famous aviator.

▶ ▶ ▶ ▶ **FIND OUT MORE** ◀ ◀ ◀
Vaudeville

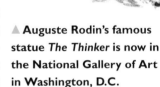

▲ **Auguste Rodin's famous statue *The Thinker* is now in the National Gallery of Art in Washington, D.C.**

▲ **The humorist Will Rogers delighted millions of people in the United States with his radio broadcasts.**

▼ Competitors in a speed skating competition. Their helmets and tight suits help lessen wind resistance. On the turns, they crouch low to reduce drag. Both men and women compete in this sport.

ROLLER-SKATING

Roller-skating is the sport in which people use wheeled boots to glide. Many years ago, young people wore skates with steel wheels that clamped to their shoes and had straps that buckled around the ankles. Special keys loosened or tightened the clamps. These skates were used outdoors only.

Today, many skaters use roller skates that have plastic, fiber, or wooden wheels. Most of these skates are used for skating on indoor roller rinks. There are two sets of wheels on each skate, attached permanently to ankle-high shoes or boots. Rubber cushions under the soles make the wheels flexible and permit the roller skaters to turn by leaning. The four-wheel type of roller skate was first patented by a New Yorker, James Plimpton, in 1867.

Indoor rinks make roller-skating a year-round pastime and sport. The rinks' floors are usually made of hardwood and are protected by a plastic finish. Often, music is played in the rink so skaters can glide along to the rhythm.

Roller-skating is a fun recreational activity, but it is also an organized, competitive sport. Athletes compete in speed skating outdoors or on rinks. *Roller derbies* are speed-skating contests on a circular track. Usually five men and five women are on each team. The roller skaters score points by passing players on the other team. The roller skaters wear pads and football helmets.

Roller-hockey, another competi-

tive sport, is much like ice hockey, but players wear roller skates. It is played with a ball instead of a puck. Each team has only five players, including one goalie.

Other roller-skating competitions are held for figure skating. Dancing and free-skating are judged in contests. Many roller skaters have created fascinating routines of spins and jumps. There are competitions for individuals and couples.

Rollerblading came about in the late 1970s. *Rollerblades* are skates with the wheels all in one row, centered in the middle of ankle-high shoe skates, much like ice skates. Most outdoor skaters today wear rollerblades. Good rollerbladers need to be very agile and have a good sense of balance. This sport has also become competitive in many parts of the world.

Skateboarding is rather like roller-skating. The skater uses a board with wheels like roller-skate wheels. Skateboarding is very popular and is performed on sidewalks and in skateboard rinks.

Roller-skating, rollerblading, and skateboarding should be done mostly on flat, smooth roads or sidewalks. You should wear gloves, knee and elbow pads, and a bicycle helmet to avoid serious injur in case of a fall.

▶ ▶ ▶ ▶ **FIND OUT MORE** ◀ ◀ ◀ ◀
Ice Hockey; Ice Skating; Sports

 ROMAN ART

The Romans made great advances in the field of architecture. They became skilled in the use of the arch, and in the use of the vault and the dome that use the arch principle to cover wide areas. As the 1,900-year-old aqueduct on the next page shows, they were good at using stone. In Rome itself, though, the Romans often used brick and concrete. These materials allowed them to create their great vaulted

▼ Skateboards were developed in California during the 1960s. These boards on wheels were used by surfers to practice when there were no waves. At first, the boards were of wood with metal wheels, but today the wheels are made of rubber and the board is usually fiberglass.

◀ The Colosseum, Rome, Italy. It was built by the Romans nearly 2,000 years ago, as a giant sports arena. Romans went to the Colosseum to see men called gladiators fighting each other or wild animals such as lions. The Colosseum was made up of many arches (which gave strength to the building) built on top of one another in a circle.

spaces. The dome of the Pantheon, a round temple, is 143 feet (43.5 m) in diameter inside. It was 1,300 years before such a dome could be built again, and this was at the Cathedral of Florence, Italy.

The Greeks disliked the arch and built with *columns* and *lintels*—posts carrying beams across their tops. But their architecture was very beautiful, and the Romans used its forms to decorate their own buildings. An archway would be framed by what seemed to be two columns and a lintel that carried the sort of decoration used in a Greek temple.

In Rome and other cities, huge buildings were erected, such as *baths* (where thousands of people came to swim and socialize), *basilicas* (where law courts and public offices were located), and *temples* (where thousands at a time met to worship). The Colosseum in the city of Rome seated about 50,000 people and contained miles of corridors and stairs to handle crowds of spectators and whole armies of performers.

The aqueduct shown here, still standing today, is one section out of thousands of miles of aqueducts built to carry water from mountain streams to cities and towns. The water flowed along a trough at the top. It had to slope gradually downward so the water would keep moving and reach the town before it evaporated. Using soldiers as a work force, Roman engineers also built roads, fortifications, harbors, and bridges.

Roman sculptors of the first century were kept busy copying Greek statues. They spent most of their time doing this, because Roman

▼ The Pont du Gard, in southern France, is a Roman bridge and *aqueduct* (waterway) built in the early 100s. It was built to supply water to the town of Nemausus (now Nimes), one of the richest towns of Roman Gaul.

▲ A Roman altar carving (from London) shows the god Mithras sacrificing a bull. The cult of Mithras was popular among Roman soldiers.

▲ The houses of wealthy Romans were richly decorated with wall paintings. This one, showing a garden, comes from the palace of Livia, the wife of the emperor Augustus. Gardens were a popular subject for these paintings; they give the impression that the solid walls of the house have melted away to reveal trees and flowers.

citizens were very fond of Greek sculpture, and those with enough money paid high prices for copies of the original statues. Eventually, this craze for Greek art died down, and Roman portrait sculpture became extremely popular. Portrait sculptors chiseled the facial features of their sculpture to look exactly like the real person they were copying. They showed every detail that made a person's face individual and unique, even wrinkles, scars, warts, or baldness.

As Rome conquered more and more territory, *narrative sculpture* became a popular art form. This type of sculpture was done on long strips of stone, where sculptors depicted entire histories of victorious battles, heroic deeds, and the lives of emperors.

Most Roman painting has been destroyed over the course of time, but paintings from the city of Pompeii still exist. Pompeii was a well-to-do coun-

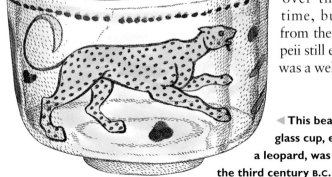

◄ This beautiful Roman glass cup, engraved with a leopard, was made during the third century B.C.

try town that was buried under lava from Mount Vesuvius, a volcano that erupted in A.D. 79. Pompeiian wall paintings were done in *fresco* (painting on damp plaster). The artists are unknown, but there is a great deal of excellent art showing scenes of home life, plants and animals, landscapes, and gods and goddesses. A fine example of a Roman wall painting showing birds, trees, and flowers is shown above. Artists in the 1700s imitated this art.

The floors and walls of many Roman houses and public buildings were covered with excellent mosaics, done with tiles, that depicted scenes similar to those of the wall paintings.

▶ ▶ ▶ ▶ **FIND OUT MORE** ◄ ◄ ◄ ◄
Building Material; Greek Art;
Mosaic; Pompeii; Rome, Ancient

ROMAN CATHOLIC CHURCH

For the first 1,000 years after the death of Jesus Christ, all Christians were members of the same religion—Christianity. There were no separate *sects*, or branches, of Christianity as there are today. The word *catholic* means "universal," and for those first 1,000 years after the death of

Jesus Christ, all Christians were members of the Catholic Church.

In 1054, however, after a long dispute between Church leaders in Rome and Constantinople (now Istanbul, Turkey), the Catholic Church split. Eastern churches under the leadership of Constantinople would not accept the bishop of Rome, known as the pope, as head of the entire Church. The Eastern churches became independent of the pope's rule and established the Orthodox Church. The Western church, under the leadership of the bishop of Rome, became known as the Roman Catholic Church. Except in the matter of papal authority, the beliefs of the Catholic and Orthodox churches are very much alike.

In 1517, another great split occurred in the Roman Catholic Church—the Protestant Reformation. Martin Luther, a German priest, and many other religious leaders *protested* against the authority of the popes and the corrupt practices of many bishops, priests, and *lay people* (those who are not members of the clergy). The Protestants *reformed* their ways of worship and started new Christian sects, such as the Lutheran, Methodist, Presbyterian, and Episcopal churches, which have since developed beliefs and practices that differ from those of the Roman Catholic Church.

However, the popes themselves realized that changes were needed. Between 1520 and 1650 the Counter Reformation corrected corrupt practices and strengthened the Roman Catholic Church.

In 1962, Pope John XXIII called together the Second Vatican Council, attended by bishops and Church leaders from all over the world. The Council made many new decisions about the practice of the Catholic faith. These decisions have led to hundreds of changes that are making Catholicism more relevant to the lives of modern-day people.

Organization of the Church

Roman Catholics believe that their religion was founded by Jesus Christ. The apostle Peter moved to Rome about A.D. 60, and became the first bishop there. From the time of Peter until today, there has been an almost unbroken line of bishops in Rome, who have been called pope (for about 70 years during the 1300s, the popes resided in Avignon, France). The word *pope* comes from the Greek word *pappas,* meaning "father." Roman Catholics believe the pope to be the visible human leader of the Church. He is believed to be the representative of Christ on Earth.

In charge of each local Catholic parish is a *pastor,* who may be assisted by one or more priests. An area that includes a large number of parishes is called a *diocese. A bishop,* appointed by the pope, heads each diocese. *Archbishops* head larger areas, called *provinces,* which contain several dioceses. *Cardinals,* who are usually bishops or archbishops, are appointed by the pope and are the pope's special advisers. When a pope dies, all the cardinals meet in Rome to elect a new pope.

▲ This jeweled cross, made in Constantinople (now Istanbul) in about A.D. 1000, shows the Virgin Mary with Saint Basil and Saint Gregory.

▼ The Council of Trent, held from 1545 to 1563, made changes to strengthen the Roman Catholic Church.

▶ **Festival and saints' days in the Roman Catholic church are often celebrated with special processions and masses. This is a confirmation procession in Switzerland.**

Pope Pius IX had the longest papal reign. He was pope from 1846 to 1878, nearly 32 years. The shortest reign was that of Pope Stephen II. He was in office for only three or four days.

▼ **Chartres cathedral in France, with its twin spires and beautiful rose window, is one of the greatest Roman Catholic cathedrals in the world. Chartres was built during the late 1100s and early 1200s.**

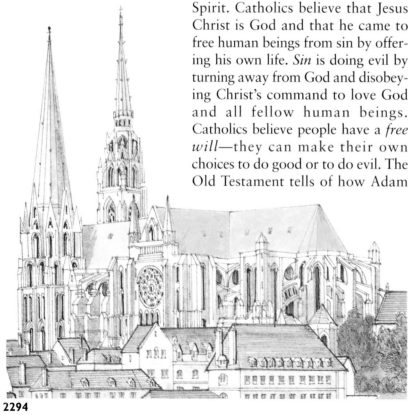

Some Roman Catholics choose to serve Christ and the Church by joining religious societies. Women who become *sisters*, or *nuns*, and men who become *brothers*, or *monks*, dedicate their lives completely to the service of God by doing good works. Some of the best-known religious societies are the Society of Jesus (the Jesuits), the Franciscans (founded by St. Francis of Assisi), the Dominicans, and the Benedictines.

Roman Catholic Faith

The faith of the Roman Catholic Church is based on scripture and on *tradition* (the teachings of Christ believed to have been handed down orally). Any teaching that is not in agreement with these two sources is not in keeping with God's word. When Roman Catholics have difficulty in agreeing whether a teaching is correct or not, the pope consults with his bishops, prays to God for guidance, and reaches a decision.

GOD AND HUMAN BEINGS. Catholics believe in the *Trinity*—three persons in one God: the Father, the Son (Jesus Christ), and the Holy Spirit. Catholics believe that Jesus Christ is God and that he came to free human beings from sin by offering his own life. *Sin* is doing evil by turning away from God and disobeying Christ's command to love God and all fellow human beings. Catholics believe people have a *free will*—they can make their own choices to do good or to do evil. The Old Testament tells of how Adam

and Eve turned against God by disobeying God's orders. Adam and Eve's action was the *original*, or first, sin. Roman Catholics believe this original sin—this tendency of a person to turn away from God—is part of imperfect human nature. Since people are not perfect, they sometimes choose to turn against God, just as Adam and Eve did in the Old Testament of the Bible.

By becoming human as Jesus Christ, God became one with mankind. By dying on the cross, God sacrificed life to make up for the sins of human beings. This means, according to Roman Catholic belief, that God now shares divine life with human beings, just as God once shared human life on Earth. God lives in all men and women through the Holy Spirit, and all people live in God through the same spirit. Each person has a personal relationship with God. And God shares life through a person's faith and actions, prayer, and the sacraments.

SACRAMENTS. The Roman Catholic Church has seven sacraments: baptism, Holy Eucharist, confirmation, reconciliation, matrimony, holy orders, and the anointing of the sick. The sacraments are visible ways in which God continues to share life with human beings. The sacraments are a source of strength to help people do God's will. This spiritual strength is called *grace*. The sacraments are also visible signs of God's presence and action in the world. Roman Catholics believe that the sacraments are actions of God working through the faith and actions of the people.

The central sacrament of the Church is the *Eucharist*, a reenacting of the Last Supper, during which Christ told his Apostles to continue to *consecrate* (make holy) bread and wine in his memory. Catholics believe that at consecration, the bread and wine become Christ's body and blood, even though they appear to be bread and wine. By taking part in the Eucharist, Catholics believe that they join their own lives with that of Christ.

▶▶▶▶ **FIND OUT MORE** ◀◀◀◀
Bible; Christianity; Clergy; Francis of Assisi; Jesus Christ; Missionary; Monastic Life; Orthodox Church; Pope; Protestant Churches; Protestant Reformation; Religion; Saint; Vatican City

ROMANCE LANGUAGES

The languages of southern Europe—French, Italian, Portuguese, and Spanish—have been grouped by linguists into a category called Romance languages. This name was given to them because they developed directly from Latin—the language spoken by the Roman people. The Roman Empire covered large areas of Europe, which included modern-day France, Italy, Portugal, and Spain.

There were two major kinds of Latin—the Latin spoken by educated people (now called Classic Latin) and the less formal Latin spoken by the common people (now called Vulgar Latin). The people of conquered countries learned the Vulgar Latin spoken by the Romans with whom they were most in contact—soldiers and traders. The Romance languages

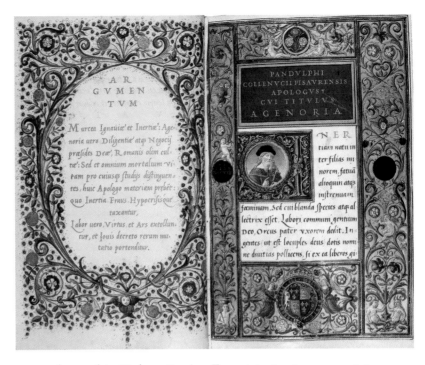

come from this Vulgar Latin. For example, although the Latin word for a horse is *equus*, the soldiers called an army horse *caballus*. In French, the general word for horse became *cheval*; in Italian, it became *cavallo*; and in Spanish, it became *caballo*.

French is the language of France, Haiti, and parts of Canada, Belgium, and Switzerland. It is also spoken in French colonies and former French colonies in Africa and the Pacific islands. The great influence of French culture in the world means that French is widely spoken in diplomatic and cultural circles. To greet someone in French you would say, *Comment allez-vous?* (KOH-mawn tahl-lay VOO? [How are you?])

Italian is more like Latin than other Romance languages, because Rome, Italy, was the capital of the Roman Empire. Many dialects, or variations, of Latin were spoken in Italy during the Roman Empire and after. It was not until the Renaissance that the Italian dialect of the city of Florence became accepted as the national language of Italy. To greet someone in Italian, you would say, *Comé stà?* (koh-may STAH? [How are you?])

▲ **Latin, the source of the Romance languages, survived as a written language long after it ceased to be spoken in everyday life. This Latin manuscript was produced in Rome in the early 1500s.**

One of the oldest Romance languages is Provençal, spoken in parts of southern France. It was in this language that the poet musicians, called *troubadours,* entertained kings, queens, and courtiers with their love songs in the 1100s and 1200s.

Portuguese is spoken not only in Portugal but also in the large South American nation of Brazil, which was colonized by the Portuguese. To greet someone in Portuguese, you would say, *Como està?* (koh-moh ayZHTAH? [How are you?])

Spanish is the national language of Spain and all the Latin American countries colonized by the Spaniards. To greet someone in Spanish you would say, *Cómo està?* (koh-moh aySTAH? [How are you?]) Other Romance, or Latinian, languages are Romanian, Catalan, Sardinian, Provençal, Romansh, Friulian, and Haitian Creole.

▶ ▶ ▶ ▶ **FIND OUT MORE** ◀ ◀ ◀ ◀
Languages; Latin; Rome, Ancient

ROMAN EMPIRE

SEE ROME, ANCIENT

ROMANESQUE ART

By A.D. 1000, Christianity was the religion of most of western Europe. Villages of humble wooden houses dotted the countryside. Among these poor homes arose mag-nificent stone churches and cathedrals. The townspeople built their churches as monuments to God. The church—its towers soaring high in the air toward heaven—was the pride of the community.

The architects of the Romanesque period (800–1200) left no written record of themselves. We do not even know their names. But we do know their magnificent stone churches. When a church was built, villagers helped quarry the stone and transport it to the building site. Traveling craftspeople cut and shaped the stones. Stonemasons put the stones in place, and traveling sculptors carved religious figures used for decoration. The building of a church took 30 to 50 years or more, depending on the size of the structure.

The word *Romanesque* means "like Roman art." Although the art does not look at all Roman, architects did design their first churches according to the floor plans of Roman buildings called *basilicas* that were used as places for transacting business. Church basilicas of the Romanesque period were rectangular in shape, with a central aisle leading to the altar. On each side of the center aisle were rows of columns and one or two side aisles. Later churches were built in the shape of a cross. The church was usually built with the altar facing east, toward the Holy Land where Christ had lived.

Roman basilicas had flat wooden roofs that were dangerous, because they burned easily. Romanesque architects built fireproof stone vaults for ceilings instead. The *barrel vault* was like a tunnel. It was easy to build, but it had to be supported by heavy walls, so churches were very dark. The *groin vault* was like a barrel vault intersected by other bar-

▼ This drawing shows the typical rectangular plan of a Romanesque cathedral, with its three towers.

rel vaults. It allowed windows to be put high in the church, because now the weight of the vaulting fell on isolated points. In place of a heavy wall, *piers* (thick columns of masonry) and *buttresses* (masonry masses that resisted sideward thrusts) took the weight of the vault. But the groin vault was complicated to build.

Romanesque churches usually contained painting and sculpture. Church sculpture was not just for decoration. It was meant to remind people of God's greatness. Every piece of sculpture had a religious meaning. The figures were carved directly onto the stones that were to be used in building the church. Craftspeople, called stonecutters, shaped each stone to fit a certain place on the building. Sculptors then carved the figures to fit the shape of the stone and the area of the building where the stone would be laid. For this reason, Romanesque sculpture does not look realistic.

In Italy, Romanesque churches did not have much sculpture. The Italians decorated the inside walls with *frescoes* (pictures painted on damp plaster) and mosaics. All the paintings and mosaics had a religious meaning, just as the sculpture did. The fresco shown here depicts a scene from the Book of Revelation in the New Testament. The 12 old men represent the elders, or wise men, of the Church. They are raising gold cups that contain the wine used at Mass. (Wine is a symbol of Christ's blood, which was shed when he died on the cross.) Above the elders is a winged ox with a book and halo. The book represents the Bible, and the ox represents St. Luke, the gospel writer. Near the top you can see part of a circle. This circle contains a lamb, which is one of the symbols of Christ. The whole scene represents the Church's adoration of Christ.

The windows of Romanesque churches were made of stained glass, in which religious scenes and people

were depicted. Such things as candlesticks, altars, chairs, and priests' clothing were all decorated with symbolic figures and objects. Most people of the Romanesque period did not know how to read or write. But almost everyone could understand religious painting and sculpture. Romanesque artists did not try to portray things as they looked in real life. They tried to portray the spiritual things of heaven.

Among the famous Romanesque cathedrals are those at Pisa in Italy, Cluny and Poitiers in France, and Santiago de Compostela in Spain.

▲ This Romanesque fresco adorns the domed ceiling over the altar of the cathedral in Anagni, Italy.

◄ The Cathedral of Durham, England, is a work of Norman (English) Romanesque. This interior view shows how a groin vault allows light to come through the clerestory windows. The vaults rest on great piers that rise from the floor in the form of clustered shafts.

▲ This mosaic in the Monreale Abbey Church in Sicily is an example of Romanesque art.

The Roman architect Vitruvius wrote about the frescoes on the walls of Roman villas: "When the plastered walls are made solid and have been polished like white marble, they will look splendid after the colors are put on. When the colors are carefully painted on damp plaster they do not fade but become permanent."

▶ ▶ ▶ ▶ **FIND OUT MORE** ◀ ◀ ◀ ◀
Cathedral; Middle Ages; Mosaic

ROMAN GODS

SEE GODS AND GODDESSES

ROMANIA

Romania is a country on the Balkan Peninsula of southeastern Europe, where the Danube River divides into several branches and then flows into the Black Sea. The river goes along Romania's western border with Serbia and its southern border with Bulgaria. Hungary lies west of Romania. Ukraine lies to the north, and Moldova lies to the east.

The highlands of the area called Transylvania, in northwestern Romania, are surrounded by the beautiful Transylvanian Alps and Carpathian mountains. Thick forests cover the mountain slopes. Between the forests, farmers tend their livestock on green pastures. The soil in the Danube River valley is among the richest in Europe. Golden fields of corn and wheat stretch from the Danube valley to the mountains. To the east are Romania's sunny beaches along the Black Sea.

Winters are cold and summers are warm in Romania. Some lowland areas (although not the seacoast and the Danube River swamps) receive little rainfall and sometimes suffer *drought* (prolonged dryness), affecting both crops and animals.

Bucharest is the capital city. It was a glamorous city before World War II, with many palaces, theaters, and luxury hotels. Today, it is the country's business and industrial center.

Romania has valuable mineral resources. It is an important producer of oil and natural gas in Europe. Coal, bauxite, iron ore, manganese, lead, and other minerals are mined. Modern factories make steel and heavy machinery. But despite all the industry in Romania, about three out of every ten Romanians are farmers.

Many Romanians are descended from the Romans who once settled this land. The name Romania comes from the Romans. Sometimes it is spelled "Rumania." Modern Romania was formed in 1859 when the old principalities of Moldavia and Walachia were joined. The country's size increased after World War I, when Transylvania, which had been part of Austria-Hungary, was added to Romania.

Romania was a socialist republic controlled by the Communist Party. At the end of World War II, Russian troops occupied Romania. In 1947, the Communist Party took over the government. Romania wanted independence from the former Soviet Union. In 1989, the people overthrew the corrupt communist government of Nicolae Ceausescu, who was executed. Romanians obtained democratic reforms and free elections. The first one, in 1990, was won by Ion Ilescu and his National Salvation Front. Romania is now striving to overcome economic problems, and to adapt to its new status as a democracy.

▶▶▶▶ **FIND OUT MORE** ◀◀◀◀
Black Sea; Danube River

music, visual art, and architecture have all been popular. The time known as the Romantic Period in art occurred mainly between the late 1700s and the mid-1800s. It started in Europe, but its influence spread to the United States, where Romanticism became important as the first U.S. art form that did not just copy the European.

What is Romanticism? It is a certain style in the arts—literature, painting, music, philosophy, sculpture, or architecture. It shows great use of the imagination and emotion. Sometimes Romantic artists put mystery and wonder into their work.

ROMANIA

Capital city
Bucharest
(2,298,000 people)

Area
91,699 square miles
(237,500 sq. km)

Population
23,278,000 people

Government
Multiparty republic

Natural resources
Oil, natural gas,
copper, iron ore

Export products
Machinery and
equipment, fuels,
minerals, metals,
manufactured
consumer goods

Unit of money
Leu

Official language
Romanian

Satu Mare • Botosani
Baia Mare • Suceava
CARPATHIAN MOUNTAINS
Oradea
Iasi
Cluj-Napoca • Piatra Neamt
APUSENI MTS.
Bacau
Tirgu Mures
Arad
Timisoara
Hunedoara • Sibiu • Moldoveanu 8,343 ft. 2,543 m. • Brasov • Focsani
Resita
TRANSYLVANIAN ALPS
Galati
Braila
Buzau
Tulcea
Rimnicu Vilcea
Tirgu Jiu • Tirgoviste • Ploiesti
Pitesti
Drobeta-Turnu Severin • Slatina • Bucharest
Craiova
Constanta
Danube
BLAC SEA

0   50   100   150 Miles
0   50   100   150   200 Kilometers
© 1994 GeoSystems, an R.R. Donnelley & Sons Company

ROMAN NUMERAL

SEE NUMBER

ROMANTIC PERIOD

Romantic art, or Romanticism, has been popular in many ages throughout history. Romantic literature,

They often paint subjects from untamed nature. Painting trees and mountains, sunsets and rivers, they can often express infinite distance, solitude, and a sense of tragedy.

The British artist Joseph M. W. Turner (1775–1851) was one of the leading Romantic painters. Turner would study the geological elements of a scene in detail, but in painting it,

Most of the oil used by the German forces in World War II came from the oil fields around Ploesti in Romania. Because of this, Ploesti was one of the targets most heavily bombed by Allied planes.

▲ *White Cloud, Head Chief of the Iowas* by George Catlin. This painting is now in the Paul Mellon Collection of the National Gallery of Art, Washington, D.C. Some U.S. writers got their romantic notions of the Native Americans from Catlin's research.

▼ *Two Men Gazing at the Moon* by Caspar David Friedrich.

he used the picture in his mind rather than the facts. Turner's influence on Romanticism was very great. His powerful imagination changed the places he saw into a fantasy world on canvas. He did historical and mythological scenes. He also liked to paint sunsets and seascapes. The picture to the right combines the two types of scenes he liked.

A later Romantic painting trend in England was the Pre-Raphaelite Brotherhood of the mid-1800s. They supported a movement to emphasize arts and crafts, and like the Romantics they longed for the past.

Romanticism spread through Europe. In Germany, Romantic painters and philosophers worked together very closely. One of the greatest German landscape painters was Caspar David Friedrich (1774–1840). Look at his picture below of *Two Men Gazing at the Moon*. Notice how the tree seems to have a personality of its own. It looks almost human. The mysterious feeling of the painting fits into the Romantic idea of mood setting. The hazy moonlight casts a ghostly light on the scene.

George Catlin (1796–1872) was the first Romantic painter in the United States. He painted pictures of

▲ *The Shipwreck* by the great English Romantic painter J.M.W. Turner.

the Native Americans and made heroes of them. He lived among the Native Americans for five years, returning East with many paintings and drawings. He wanted to portray the Native Americans before they all disappeared from the frontier. Shown here is a portrait called *White Cloud, Head Chief of the Iowas*. As a Romantic, Catlin shows the Chief in a rather mysterious, wondrous way.

The vast, untouched beauty of the North American wilderness appealed to U.S. Romantic painters. They felt that a landscape should be transfigured and lit up by the spirit of the painter. This was true of the work of Thomas Cole (1801–1848). Cole studied in Europe, and when he came back, he introduced the symbolic landscape to the United States. He loved the wild, primitive character of the U.S. countryside and tried to show it in his pictures. He felt that people in Europe had tamed the countryside too much, but the United States was still an untouched territory. A whole group of U.S. Romantics, known as the Hudson River School, became prominent painters in the mid-1800s. Some art critics today say that some of the finest Romantic paintings of the 1800s were created by U.S. painters.

▶▶▶▶ **FIND OUT MORE** ◀◀◀◀
Art History

ROME

Rome, as the capital of the Roman Empire, was for five centuries the center of the Western world. Rome has been one of the major centers of civilization for more than 2,000 years. It is often called the Eternal City.

According to legend, Rome was founded by twins named Romulus and Remus in about 750 B.C. The city was built on the banks of the Tiber River in central Italy. It grew to become the center of the vast Roman Empire. The Romans built many magnificent buildings on the seven hills that made up the ancient city. The ruins of some of these are still standing. The *Colosseum* is a huge arena where Roman gladiators once fought, and where early Christians were killed because of their religion. The *catacombs* are underground caves and tunnels where these early Christians hid and practiced their religion. The caves contain chapels, meeting halls, and tombs. The *Forum* was the center of government and business life.

After the collapse of the Roman Empire, many of the Roman buildings were taken apart to use for building material. Wild Germanic tribes occupied Rome, and it became an area of ruined buildings and unhealthy swamps. The bishops of Rome (later called the popes) became the leaders of the city during this unsettled time. The popes built many churches in the city in the 1500s and 1600s. In 1929, the Italian government gave an area in the city to the pope. This area, called Vatican City, is actually an independent state.

Today, many visitors come to Rome to see the ancient ruins and the beautiful churches. But the city is also important for its modern achievements. It is the capital of Italy and the home of almost three million people. It is also an international center for motion-picture production and fashion design.

▶ ▶ ▶ ▶ **FIND OUT MORE** ◀ ◀ ◀ ◀
Christianity; Italian History; Italy; Pope; Roman Catholic Church; Rome, Ancient; Vatican City

▲ **The modern city of Rome. This is a view over St. Peter's square from the dome of St. Peter's basilica.**

ROME, ANCIENT

In its earliest days, Rome was a small town built upon seven hills. It lay near the mouth of the Tiber River in Italy. Rome later grew into a mighty city, which ruled an empire. The Roman Empire, at its largest, covered more than 2 million square miles (5 million sq. km). More than 50 million people lived in it.

A Time of Legend (700–509 B.C.)

The first Romans were probably made up of three different peoples: the Latins, the Sabines, and the Etruscans. A well-known legend tells how twin boys named Romulus and Remus were born in Italy in the 700s B.C. Their mother was a Latin princess, descended from a mighty warrior, Aeneas. Their father was Mars, god of war. The boys were abandoned as infants. A she-wolf nursed them, and a farmer raised them. When they were grown, the twins founded the city of Rome on the Palatine Hill, one of the seven hills of Rome. Romulus became

▲ **The symbol of Rome was the she-wolf, which according to legend, adopted the twin brothers Romulus and Remus. When the boys grew up, they decided to found a city, but they quarreled. Romulus killed Remus and founded the city, later named "Rome" after himself.**

THE ROMAN EMPIRE— KEY DATES

B.C. 900s Rise of Etruscans in northern Italy.

753 According to legend, the year in which Romulus founded the city of Rome.

509 Founding of the Roman Republic.

264–201 Rome defeats Carthage (a city in North Africa) in the first two Punic Wars, and gains its first overseas territories.

149–146 The Third Punic War, which ended with the destruction of Carthage.

133–60 Aristocratic (*patrician*) and popular (*plebeian*) parties struggle for power.

59–52 Julius Caesar conquers Gaul.

49–44 Julius Caesar is Rome's dictator.

44 Julius Caesar is assassinated, and Rome is ruled by three men together: Lepidus, Mark Antony, and Octavian (Caesar's grandnephew).

27 Octavian becomes the first emperor and is named Augustus.

A.D. 293 Diocletian divides the empire into two sections, east and west.

313 Constantine the Great and Licinius declare that Christianity should be tolerated throughout the empire.

324 Constantine puts Licinius to death and reunites the empire.

476 The last western emperor (Romulus Augustulus) is deposed.

1453 Constantinople falls to the Ottoman Turks, signifying the end of the Eastern Empire.

Rome's first king in 753 B.C. and gave his name to the city. According to tradition, six other kings ruled after Romulus. The last of these was Tarquinius Superbus (often called "Tarquin the Proud"). He was a harsh, cruel tyrant and was overthrown in 509 B.C.

The Roman Republic (509–27 B.C.)

Rome then became a *republic*. In a republic, citizens may vote for the governors of their choice. The Romans chose two persons called *consuls* to rule the republic. Consuls could remain in office for only one year. An assembly, called the *senate*, was made up of people who acted as advisers to the consuls. Throughout much of Rome's history, the Roman people were divided into two main classes—*patricians* and *plebeians*. The patricians were members of noble Roman families. The plebeians were the common people—most of the population. After a long struggle, the plebeians gained equal power in the government.

By the middle of the 200s B.C., the Romans had taken over most of Italy. In 264 B.C., Rome went to war with the powerful city of Carthage, in North Africa. Rome fought three wars with Carthage, known as the *Punic Wars*. By 146 B.C., Carthage had been totally destroyed. The Romans conquered Spain, Macedonia, Greece, and much of the Middle East. They later moved into Gaul (now France).

In 70 B.C., Pompey the Great was made consul. He formed a *triumvirate* (three-person government) with two other Roman statesmen, Julius Caesar and Crassus. After the deaths of Crassus and Pompey, Julius Caesar ruled alone. He was a brilliant leader, both in war and at home. But some people feared that he would become too powerful and make himself emperor. In 44 B.C., he was stabbed to death in Rome.

Another triumvirate was formed by Caesar's grandnephew Octavian (also called Augustus), a commander named Lepidus, and Mark Antony, a

▲ The Senate was the governing council of the Roman republic. It consisted of a group of elders who elected two consuls each year to lead them.

young politician and general. Lepidus soon fell from power, and the rule was divided between Antony and Octavian. Antony was married to Octavian's sister, but he divorced his wife to marry Cleopatra, queen of Egypt. Octavian declared war on both of them. Cleopatra and Antony were defeated by Octavian's army, and they killed themselves in 31 B.C. Octavian then became supreme ruler of Rome and its territories.

Rome Becomes an Empire (27 B.C.–A.D. 180)

Octavian was the first Roman emperor. He had earlier taken the name of his great uncle, and *Caesar* became a Roman word for "emperor." Octavian was also named Augustus, meaning "revered one." In A.D. 14, his stepson, Tiberius, became emperor. The next emperor, Caligula, was insane and was killed by his own guards. Nero, also probably insane, was condemned to death by the senate for his cruel ways and killed himself in A.D. 68. Vespasian and his two sons followed one another as emperors from 69 to 96. The age of the "five good emperors" came next. They were Nerva, Trajan, Hadrian, Antoninus Pius, and Marcus Aurelius. During their reigns, the Roman Empire reached its greatest size. In A.D. 117, the boundaries of the empire stretched north and south from Britain to Egypt, and east and west from Spain to Armenia. It included 43 *provinces,* or districts, under Roman rule.

The End of the Empire
(A.D 180–476)

Marcus Aurelius died in A.D. 180, and his son Commodus was named emperor. Like Caligula and Nero, Commodus was insane. He was murdered. The office of emperor had been dragged so low that it was even auctioned off to the highest bidder.

Barbarian tribes were attacking the Roman borders. A large and costly army was needed to defend the enormous empire. Roman citizens were forced to pay higher and higher taxes. Prices rose so much that few people could buy bread. The Romans suffered from plagues and began to die of starvation. In the 200s, many emperors came to power, but most were either weak or vicious. Several more emperors were murdered. In A.D. 284, Diocletian became emperor. His efforts to protect the borders from the barbarians saved the empire for a few more years.

Constantine, whose reign began in A.D. 312, was the last of the great Roman emperors. Constantine was the first Christian emperor. He made Christianity the official religion of the Roman Empire. Before this time, the Romans had worshiped many gods. In A.D. 330, Constantine founded a new capital city of Byzantium, later renamed Constantinople

(now Istanbul, Turkey). The empire had been divided into two parts. Rome remained the center of the Western Empire. But the Eastern Empire, with its capital at Constantinople, became much more powerful. For 1,100 more years, Eastern Roman, or Byzantine, emperors ruled from Constantinople.

The city of Rome, left almost deserted, was attacked again and again by invading barbarians. In A.D. 410, Visigoths captured and sacked Rome. The last Western Roman emperor was Romulus Augustulus. A barbarian leader, Odoacer, overthrew him in A.D. 476. Odoacer then became king of Italy. The end of the Roman Empire had come.

The Roman People

What were they like, those long-ago Romans? They built magnificent government buildings, temples, bridges, roads, and *aqueducts* (waterways). They invented a very strong type of concrete, which they used to build impressive arches and domes. More than 50,000 miles (80,000 km) of Roman roads carried traders and armies throughout the empire. The Romans developed a system of law on which many of our own modern laws are based. They believed that laws were made for the good of the people and that all individuals had rights—unless they were slaves.

Loose robes called *togas* were worn by Roman men. Women wore long, straight dresses called *stolas,* and both men and women wore sandals. Men and women spent many hours at the *baths.* The famed Roman baths had hot and cold bath areas, steam rooms, dining rooms, music rooms, rooms for playing games, and even libraries.

▲ A Roman legionary soldier. The power of ancient Rome was based on its efficient, professional army.

QUIZ
1. What river runs through Rome?
2. What was the Roman *triumvirate?*
3. When was the Roman Republic founded?
4. Who were the "five good emperors"?
5. What *legacy* (inventions, etc.) did the ancient Romans leave to civilization?
(Answers on page 2304)

The Romans were the greatest road builders of the ancient world. They laid out more than 50,000 miles (80,000 km) of road across their huge empire. The best roads were wonderful feats of engineering. They had thick beds more than 3 feet (1 m) deep made of rock slabs, stones, gravel, and sand layers.

The Romans celebrated many holidays during the year. Free entertainment was provided for everyone on these days. In Rome, a huge arena called the Colosseum held about 50,000 people. Men called *gladiators* fought with one another or with wild animals in the arena. Criminals were sometimes fed to lions. Thoughtful people were horrified at the brutal spectacles, and in A.D. 404 the bloodthirsty entertainment was stopped. Another favorite amusement was the circus. The Circus Maximus in Rome seated almost 260,000 people. It offered animal acts, acrobats, clowns, and exciting, dangerous chariot races. *Chariots* were two-wheeled carts drawn by two to eight horses.

Roman soldiers were almost unbeatable professional fighters. They invented many new ways of winning battles. When the Romans took over a country, they sent a Roman *governor* to rule the people. They usually allowed the people of the conquered country to keep their own religion and speak their own language. But most people in the empire learned the Roman language, Latin. Some even became Roman citizens.

Rome produced many fine writers. Livy wrote a history of Rome. Virgil, Horace, and Ovid were three of the ancient world's greatest poets. Pliny the Elder wrote a 37-volume work on natural history. The Romans often copied the best of what they found in the lands they conquered. They adopted many ideas from the Greeks, whom they greatly admired. The Romans helped to keep alive these ideas by spreading them all over the world.

▶▶▶▶ **FIND OUT MORE** ◀◀◀◀

Byzantine Empire; Caesar, Julius; Carthage; Chariot; Christianity; Circus; Cleopatra; Gladiator; Greece, Ancient; Italian History; Latin; Law; Nero; Roman Art; Romance Languages; Rome

---

QUIZ ANSWERS

Railroad quiz, page 2215

1. Train cars and locomotives are the rolling stock of the railroads.

2. Dispatchers are in charge of all train routes and signals.

3. The Centralized Traffic Control (CTC) system is the modern way of handling railroad communications.

4. A train's locomotive consists of the engine and a cab for the engineer.

5. The first coast-to-coast railroad line in the U.S. was completed in 1869.

Religion quiz, page 2241

1. The three basic kinds of religious belief are *animism* (the earliest kind)—a belief that all natural things have souls; *polytheism*—belief in many gods; and *monotheism*—belief in one "omnipotent" (all-powerful) god.

2. Muhammad founded the Muslim religion, Islam, in the 600s.

3. Baptists, Episcopalians, Greek Orthodox, Lutherans, Methodists, Mormons, Pentecostal, Presbyterians, Congregationalists, Roman Catholics, and Russian Orthodox are some examples of Christian sects.

4. A *shaman* is a medicine man or witch doctor who (it is believed by those who follow animistic spirit religions) has magical powers such as being able to change himself into an animal or to speak with the forces of nature on his people's behalf.

5. The *Bhagavad-Gita* is the holy book of Hinduism.

Rocket quiz, page 2283

1. Rockets use a propellant that burns to push them swiftly through the atmosphere.

2. Liquid propellants are better, because they usually perform better, are more powerful, and are easier to control.

3. Dr. Robert Goddard built the first liquid-fuel rocket (in 1926).

4. The Soviet *Sputnik* I (1957) was the first man-made satellite launched by rocket.

5. The Space Shuttle made its first flight in 1981.

Rome, Ancient quiz, page 2303

1. The Tiber River (known as the *Tivere* in Italian) runs through Rome.

2. The Roman triumvirate was the three-person rulership of the Roman Republic. It was first formed in 70 B.C. by Pompey the Great, who went on to rule jointly with the statesmen Julius Caesar and Crassus.

3. The Roman Republic was founded in 509 B.C.

4. The "five good emperors" were Nerva (A.D. 96–98), Trajan (A.D 98–117), Hadrian (A.D 117–138), Antoninus Pius (A.D 138–161), and Marcus Aurelius (A.D 161–180). Together they served for a total of 84 years.

5. The Romans were great engineers. They left many wonderful buildings, bridges, roads, and systems of irrigation. Also, their system of law and government has served as a model for modern democracies. The ancient Romans also produced some of the finest art and literature in the history of the Western world.